Mama's Tea Cakes

Mama's Tea Cakes

101
Soul Food Desserts

WILBERT JONES

A BIRCH LANE PRESS BOOK

Published by
Carol Publishing Group

Designed by Deborah Kerner

A Birch Lane Press Book
Published by Carol Publishing Group
Birch Lane Press is a registered trademark of Carol Communications, Inc.

Editorial, sales and distribution, rights and permissions inquiries should be addressed to
Carol Publishing Group, 120 Enterprise Avenue, Secaucus, N.J. 07094

In Canada: Canadian Manda Group, One Atlantic Avenue, Suite 105, Toronto,
Ontario M6K 3E7

Carol Publishing books may be purchased in bulk at special discounts for sales promotion,
fundraising, or educational purposes. Special editions can be created to specifications.
For details, contact: Special Sales Department, 120 Enterprise Avenue, Secaucus, N.J. 07094.

Manufactured in the United States of America
10 9 8 7 6 5 4 3 2 1

Library of Congress Cataloging-in-Publication Data

Jones, Wilbert.
Mama's tea cakes : 101 soul food desserts / Wilbert Jones.
p.   cm.
"A Birch Lane Press book."
Includes index.
ISBN 1–55972–464–1 (hc)
1. Desserts.   2. Afro-American cookery.   I. Title.
TX773.J695   1998
641.8'6'08996073—dc21   98–4654
CIP

Contents

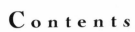

Acknowledgments

A big thanks to my mother; without her help, this book would not have been possible.

Thanks to my friends for providing such great support throughout the years—Tina Wilson, Materesa Marshall, Jason and Gwen Swackhamer, Ramona Douglass, Kina Denton, Eric Weinman, Maria Alamo-Cameron, Ann McFadden, and my wonderful cousin, Christine Randle.

Great appreciation goes to Rhonda Winchell, my agent, and Monica Harris, my editor.

Special thanks to KitchenAid and Nielsen-Massey Vanillas, Inc. for providing great products and support for this project.

Introduction

Growing up in Chicago, I could not wait for Sundays; that was when my mother would prepare some of the most awesome soul food dinners. On any given Sunday, my sisters, brother, and I would feast on homemade Parker House rolls, fried green tomatoes, green onion salad, smothered chicken, red beans and rice, twice-baked potatoes, fried corn, and pound cake. My mother's dinners were always fresh and tasty but her desserts were especially memorable. My favorites were Sweet Potato Pie (p. 66), German Sweet Chocolate Cake (p. 24), and mother's homemade Vanilla Ice Cream (p. 116).

As an adult, I continue to prepare and enjoy these desserts that are not only rich in flavor but in African-American history, the source of so many of these great recipes created by cooks on Southern plantations.

Although we are a long way from plantation life, these recipes remain part of African-American culture. The preparation of these desserts reminds one not only of the past, but of warm feelings of family and friendship. These desserts were made to ease the hardship of a long workday by ending it with something sweet. They also were used to celebrate nuptials, welcome new neighbors, comfort the bereaved, and make farewells.

Mama's Tea Cakes: 101 Delicious Soul Food Desserts restores these long lost dessert recipes and adapts them to the modern kitchen. This is the first soul food dessert cookbook. Use *Mama's Tea Cakes* to help you tempt your guests with Peach Cobbler (p. 95) at a Sunday brunch after church. Create Old-Fashioned Pound Cake (p. 30) to share at afternoon lunches with friends. End family dinners with Sweet Potato Pie (p. 66) and other delicious, mouth-watering, going-back-for-seconds desserts.

I hope you enjoy them.

Wilbert Jones

Cakes, Cakes, Cakes

There are two basic classifications of cake: Butter-based cake and sponge cake. Most soul food desserts are made from butter-based cakes, which include pound cake, fig cake, coconut cake, and sweet potato cake.

The most important aspects of cake baking is the selection of the ingredients.

Flour   A good all-purpose flour can be used as a substitute for expensive cake flour. In a substitution, use two tablespoons less per cup.

Butter   A good grade of butter gives a fine flavor to cakes.

Eggs   Eggs should be fresh and have a good flavor and odor. Always bring eggs to room temperature before using them.

Leavening   Baking powder, baking soda, and beaten egg whites are the leavening agents used in cake making.

Flavoring   Always use the best flavoring extracts in cakes. A good extract will produce a good flavor in the finished product.

Apple Pecan Layer Cake

Pecans were first called hickory nuts in the South because of their resemblance to walnuts. Although they are very tasty, shelled or unshelled pecans turn rancid easily. Shelled pecans will last up to one month in a cool place, whereas unshelled pecans last up to three months in a cool place.

3 cups all-purpose flour, sifted

2 cups sugar

1 ½ teaspoons baking powder

¼ teaspoon salt

1 teaspoon ground allspice

2 cups unsweetened applesauce

3 large eggs, slightly beaten at room temperature

½ cup vegetable oil

½ cup pecans, chopped

Preheat oven to 350° F. Combine the flour, sugar, baking powder, salt, and allspice in a medium mixing bowl. Using a whisk, mix well for one minute. Add the applesauce, eggs, and vegetable oil. Mix well with an electric mixer on medium speed for 3 minutes or until the batter is smooth. Stir in the pecans.

Pour the batter into two 9 × 1½-inch non-stick round baking pans. Bake for 30 minutes or until a toothpick inserted into the center comes out clean. Remove the cakes from the pans and let them cool for 10 minutes on wire racks before frosting.

To decorate, place one cake layer upside down on a serving plate. Spread about ¼ of the frosting evenly. Add the second cake on top (right side up). Cover the sides and top of the cake with the remaining frosting. *Serves 12.*

Frosting

4 cups powdered sugar, sifted

¼ cup (½ stick) unsalted butter, softened

4 tablespoons unsweetened apple juice

2 teaspoons vanilla extract

Place the sugar, butter, apple juice, and vanilla in a medium mixing bowl. Mix with an electric mixer on medium speed for 1 minute or until the frosting becomes spreadable. *Makes 1¼ cups of frosting.*

Banana Layer Cake

A trick for getting bananas to ripen quickly is to place them in a closed paper bag or refrigerate them overnight. Although the skin will turn black, the banana will remain sweet and firm.

2 cups all-purpose flour, sifted	½ cup buttermilk
1 ½ teaspoons baking soda	½ cup vegetable shortening
1 cup (about 1 or 2 bananas) mashed ripe banana	1 ½ cups sugar
1 teaspoon freshly squeezed lemon juice	2 large eggs, at room temperature
	1 teaspoon vanilla extract

Preheat oven to 350° F. Combine the flour and baking soda in a medium mixing bowl and mix with a wire whisk; set aside.

In a separate mixing bowl, combine banana, lemon juice, and buttermilk; beat with an electric mixer for two minutes. Add shortening and sugar, continuing to mix until creamy. Add the eggs one at a time, and stir in the vanilla.

Pour the banana mixture into the dry ingredients and beat until the batter is smooth.

Pour the batter into two 9 × 1½-inch nonstick round baking pans. Bake for 30 minutes, or until a toothpick inserted into the center comes out clean. Remove the cakes from pans and let them cool on wire racks for 10 minutes before frosting.

To decorate, place one cake layer upside down on a serving plate and spread ¼ of the frosting evenly. Add second cake on top (right side up). Cover the sides and top of the cake with the remaining frosting. *Serves 12.*

Yellow Frosting

3 egg whites, at room
   temperature
1 cup sugar
2 teaspoons vanilla extract

½ teaspoon salt
3 tablespoons water
2 drops yellow food coloring

Place the egg whites in a small copper bowl and beat with a wire whisk until stiff. Fold in the sugar, vanilla, salt, water, and food coloring. Refrigerate until ready to use. *Makes about 2 cups of frosting.*

Blackberry Jam Cake

Blackberries grow wild throughout the South. These are often picked and made into homemade jams and jellies. Blackberries are also used as main ingredients in cakes, tarts, and cobblers.

2 cups all-purpose flour, sifted
2 cups sugar
2 ½ teaspoons baking powder
1 ½ cups heavy cream
½ cup (1 stick) unsalted butter, softened

2 teaspoons vanilla extract
2 large eggs, at room temperature

Preheat oven to 350° F. Combine the flour, sugar, baking powder, cream, butter, and vanilla in a medium mixing bowl. Mix well with an electric mixer on low speed for about 3 minutes. Add the eggs and continue to mix until the batter is smooth. Pour the batter into two 9 × 1½-inch nonstick baking pans. Bake for 30 minutes or until a toothpick inserted into the center comes out clean. Remove the cakes from pans and place them on wire racks, and let them cool for 10 minutes before adding the blackberry topping.

To decorate, place one cake layer upside down on a serving plate and spread about ½ of the topping evenly over it. Add the second cake on top (right side up). Spread the remaining topping on top of the cake. Sprinkle the top and sides of the cake with powdered sugar. *Serves 6–8.*

Blackberry Topping

3 cups seedless blackberry jam   *1 tablespoon powdered sugar*
1 tablespoon fresh lemon juice

Pour the jam and lemon juice into a small saucepan. Cook the mixture for 10 minutes, stirring constantly, over low heat and until it turns into a thick syrup; remove it from the heat and let cool for 5 minutes before using.

Black and White Cake

The Black and White Cake was popular in African-American households during the Christmas season. People would frequently say, "How could something so different taste so good?"

½ cup (1 stick) unsalted butter, softened

1 cup sugar

2 large eggs, at room temperature

2 cups all-purpose flour, sifted

3 teaspoons baking powder

1 ½ cups milk

1 teaspoon vanilla extract

1 ½ tablespoons unsweetened cocoa powder

Preheat oven to 350° F. Combine the butter and sugar in a medium mixing bowl and cream with an electric mixer for 2 minutes. Beat in the eggs one at a time.

In a separate bowl, mix the flour and baking powder together. Slowly add flour mixture to the creamed butter mixture, alternating with the milk and vanilla. Mix well until the batter is smooth.

Divide batter in half, using separate bowls. Add the cocoa to one of the halves and mix it in. Pour each batch of batter into a separate 9 × 1½-inch nonstick baking pan.

Bake the cakes for 30 minutes or until a toothpick inserted into the center comes out clean. Place the cakes on wire racks and let them cool for 10 minutes before frosting.

To decorate, place the dark cake upside down on a serving plate and spread it evenly with about ¼ of the frosting. Add the white layer on top (right side up). Cover the sides and top of the cake with the remaining frosting. *Serves 12.*

Chocolate Frosting

2 one-ounce squares semisweet
  chocolate

1 14-ounce can condensed milk
1 teaspoon vanilla extract

Melt the chocolate in a double boiler. Add the milk and heat for 5 minutes, stirring constantly, until the mixture turns thick. Stir in the vanilla. *Makes about 1½ cups.*

Busy Day Cake

This quick and easy cake got its name from homemakers and mothers who had very busy schedules doing the work around the home.

3 cups all-purpose flour, sifted

4 teaspoons baking powder

2 cups granulated sugar

½ cup (1 stick) salted butter

3 large eggs, well beaten at room temperature

1 ½ cup milk

2 teaspoons vanilla extract

1 teaspoon powdered sugar

1 teaspoon cocoa powder

Preheat oven to 350° F. Combine the flour, baking powder, and sugar in a large mixing bowl. Add the butter, eggs, milk, and vanilla, and beat with an electric mixer on medium speed for about 4 minutes or until the batter is smooth.

Pour the batter into a nonstick 10-inch nonstick Bundt pan. Bake for 90 minutes or until a toothpick inserted into the center comes out clean.

Remove the cake from the oven and let cool for 10 minutes. Remove the cake from the pan and place on a wire rack. Sprinkle with powdered sugar and cocoa powder. *Serves 12.*

Caramel-Pecan Cake

Chopped walnuts can be used as a substitute for chopped pecans. If possible, use fresh walnuts; the taste will be far superior to that of packaged nuts.

1 ½ cups (3 sticks) unsalted
    butter, softened
2 cups sugar
6 large eggs, room temperature
3 cups all-purpose flour

1 ½ teaspoons baking powder
½ teaspoon salt
1 cup milk
1 teaspoon vanilla extract

Preheat oven to 350° F. Place butter and sugar in a medium mixing bowl and cream with an electric mixer for 2 minutes, or until fluffy. Beat in the eggs one at a time.

In a separate medium mixing bowl, sift flour, baking powder, and salt. Combine flour mixture with the creamed butter, alternating with the milk and vanilla. Mix for 2 minutes or until the batter is smooth.

Pour the batter into a 10-inch nonstick Bundt pan. Bake for 90 minutes or until a toothpick inserted into the center comes out clean.

To decorate, place cake on a serving plate and spread frosting on top and sides. *Serves 12.*

Frosting

3 cups sugar

¾ cup milk

½ cup (1 stick) unsalted butter

½ cup chopped pecans

2 teaspoons vanilla extract

Caramelize one cup of sugar in a medium saucepan over medium heat. Mix the remaining 2 cups of sugar and milk in another saucepan. Bring the milk to a rolling boil and pour it over the caramelized sugar, stirring constantly. Cook for about 3 minutes or until it comes to soft ball stage. Add the butter, pecans, and vanilla. Remove the frosting from heat and beat it with an electric mixer until combined.

Cola Cake

The cola cake recipe was first created in Atlanta when the Coca-Cola processing plant first opened. The recipe eventually spread throughout the South. This recipe is quite close to the original version of the Coca-Cola cake.

1 cup (2 sticks) unsalted butter, softened

1 ½ cups sugar

2 large eggs, at room temperature

½ cup buttermilk

2 cups all-purpose flour, sifted

1 teaspoon baking soda

2 tablespoons unsweetened cocoa powder

1 teaspoon vanilla extract

1 ½ cups mini marshmallows

Preheat oven to 350° F. Place the butter and sugar in a medium mixing bowl and beat with an electric mixer for 2 minutes. Add the eggs and buttermilk, mixing until the batter is smooth. In a separate medium mixing bowl, sift the flour, baking soda, and cocoa powder together. Add the flour mixture and vanilla to the batter. Fold in the marshmallows. Pour the batter into a 10-inch nonstick Bundt pan and bake for 45 minutes or until a toothpick inserted into the center comes out clean.

To decorate, spread icing on top of the cake and let it drizzle down the sides. *Serves 10–12.*

Icing

½ cup (1 stick) unsalted butter, softened

¼ cup unsweetened cocoa powder

½ cup cola

4 cups powdered sugar

Combine all the ingredients in a medium mixing bowl. Mix well with an electric mixer on low speed for 2 minutes or until icing is smooth and spreadable. *Makes about 2½ cups.*

Chocolate Fudge Loaf

For a richer flavor and firmer texture, chill the loaf in the refrigerator for at least 3 hours before serving. The texture will resemble thick chocolate fudge.

2 cups sugar	¼ cup unsweetened cocoa powder
2 cups all-purpose flour	1 cup water
1 teaspoon baking soda	1 cup heavy cream
½ cup (1 stick) unsalted butter, softened	2 large eggs, at room temperature
½ cup vegetable shortening	1 ½ teaspoons vanilla extract

Preheat oven to 325° F. Sift sugar, flour, and baking soda together in a medium mixing bowl.

Place the butter, shortening, cocoa, and water in a small saucepan and bring it to a boil, stirring constantly. Pour cocoa mixture into flour mixture, and add the cream.

Using an electric mixer, mix well and let cool. Beat in the eggs and vanilla.

Pour the batter into a 9 × 5-inch nonstick loaf pan. Bake for 45 minutes or until a toothpick inserted into the center comes out clean. Leave the cake in the pan and add the icing while the icing is still hot. Let the loaf cool for about 15 minutes, then place it in the refrigerator for 3 hours before serving. *Serves 8–10.*

Icing

½ cup (1 stick) unsalted butter
⅓ cup unsweetened cocoa
   powder

¼ cup buttermilk
1 cup powdered sugar
1 teaspoon vanilla extract

Mix the butter, cocoa, and buttermilk in a small saucepan, and bring to a rolling boil. Sift the sugar into the chocolate mixture, stirring constantly. Add the vanilla. Pour the icing over the hot Chocolate Fudge Loaf. *Makes about 1¾ cups.*

Apple Cake

This recipe can be made with fresh pears or peaches instead of fresh tart apples.

2 large eggs, at room
temperature
½ cup granulated sugar
1 cup all-purpose flour
1 ½ teaspoons baking powder
1 cup (2 sticks) unsalted
butter, softened

3 cups peeled, cored, and cubed
tart apples
1 ½ teaspoons bourbon
1 teaspoon powdered sugar

Preheat oven to 375° F. Butter the bottom and sides of a 9-inch round cake pan. Coat pan with 1 tablespoon of flour and 1 tablespoon of sugar (discard the excess).

Place the eggs in a medium mixing bowl with the sugar and beat with a wire whisk until they are thick and light. Sift the flour and baking powder together and stir it into the egg mixture. Stir in the butter and apples, and add the bourbon.

Spoon the batter into the cake pan and bake for 40 minutes or until a toothpick inserted into the center comes out clean. Let the cake cool for 10 minutes before removing it from the pan. Once cool, sprinkle it with powdered sugar. *Serves 8.*

Quick Spice Cake

This cake is an inexpensive dessert that was used when there were no chocolate or fruit preserves on hand in the household.

3 cups all-purpose flour
1 teaspoon baking soda
½ teaspoon salt
1 teaspoon ground nutmeg
½ teaspoon ground cinnamon
¼ teaspoon ground cloves
1 cup granulated sugar

1 cup light brown sugar
1 ½ cups buttermilk
1 cup (2 sticks) salted butter, softened
3 large eggs, at room temperature

Preheat oven to 350° F. Sift all the dry ingredients together in a large mixing bowl. Add the two sugars, the butter, and buttermilk, and beat with an electric mixer on medium speed until batter is well mixed. Add the eggs one at a time and mix for 2 minutes.

Pour batter into a 10-inch nonstick tube pan and bake for 90 minutes or until a toothpick inserted into the center comes out clean. Let the cake cool for 5 minutes, then remove it from the pan and place it on a serving plate. *Makes 10–12 servings.*

Fig Preserve Cake

Years ago, before fruit preserves were manufactured by large food companies, making them from scratch was very labor intensive. The process would usually take an entire day. Now the rule of thumb is to purchase fruit preserves from the grocery store — they taste great, and save a lot of time!

2 cups all-purpose flour
1 ½ teaspoons ground cloves
2 teaspoons ground cinnamon
2 teaspoons ground nutmeg
1 ½ teaspoons baking soda
1 teaspoon salt
1 ½ cups sugar

3 large eggs, at room temperature
½ cup whipping cream
½ cup canola oil
½ cup chopped pecans
1 ½ cups fig preserves, chopped

Preheat oven to 325° F. Sift together all the dry ingredients in a large mixing bowl. Add the eggs one at a time and beat well with an electric mixer. Add the cream and oil and continue to beat. Fold in pecans and fig preserves.

Pour the batter into a 9 × 13-inch nonstick baking pan. Bake for 40 minutes or until a toothpick inserted into the center comes out clean. Let the cake cool in the pan for 10 minutes before removing it. *Serves 8–10.*

Fresh Coconut Cake

Because fresh coconut was rarely available, this delicious cake was usually prepared only for very special occasions such as weddings, holidays, church dinners, and funerals.

2 cups all-purpose flour

2 teaspoons baking powder

1 cup (2 sticks) unsalted butter, softened

1 cup sugar

3 egg yolks, well beaten at room temperature

½ cup milk

3 egg whites, stiffly beaten

1 ½ teaspoons vanilla extract

Preheat oven to 375° F. Sift the flour and baking powder together in a medium mixing bowl. In a separate bowl, cream butter and sugar together with an electric mixer until light and fluffy. Add the egg yolks, alternating with the milk, to the flour mixture. Combine the flour mixture with the creamed butter mixture and mix well for 2 minutes or until batter is combined. Fold in the egg whites and vanilla.

Pour the batter into two 9-inch nonstick pans. Bake for 30 minutes or until a toothpick inserted into the center comes out clean. Let the cakes cool for 5 minutes, then remove them from the pans and place them on wire racks.

To decorate, place one cake layer upside down on a serving plate. Spread about ¼ of the frosting evenly over this layer and sprinkle about ¼ of the coconut on top. Add the second cake on top (right side up). Spread remaining frosting on the top and sides of the cake, then sprinkle with coconut. *Serves 8–10.*

Frosting

2 *egg whites, at room*
   temperature
1 ½ *cups sugar*
¼ *cup water*
2 *teaspoons light corn syrup*

1 *teaspoon vanilla extract*
1 ½ *cups freshly shredded coconut*
   mixed with 1 tablespoon
   sugar

Combine egg whites, sugar, water, and syrup in the top of a double boiler, beating with a wire whisk until thoroughly mixed. Place over rapidly boiling water and beat constantly with a whisk for about 4 minutes or until the frosting stands in peaks. Remove the mixture from the boiling water, add the vanilla, and continue to whisk until the mixture is thick enough to spread. *Makes about 3 cups.*

Georgia Pecan Cake

Although Georgia is the pecan capital of the United States, Southern states such as Mississippi, Texas, Alabama, and Louisiana continue to produce great amounts of pecans. This cake's name, however, remains the same throughout the entire country.

2 cups (4 sticks) unsalted
butter, softened
2 ½ cups sugar
6 large eggs, at room
temperature

3 cups flour, sifted
1 ½ cups buttermilk
2 cups chopped pecans
1 tablespoon vanilla extract

Preheat oven to 325° F. In a medium mixing bowl, cream the butter and sugar until fluffy using an electric mixer. Mix in the eggs one at a time for one minute each. Gradually add the flour, alternating with the buttermilk and mix until the batter is smooth. Fold in the pecans and vanilla.

Pour batter into a 10-inch nonstick tube pan. Bake for 90 minutes or until a toothpick inserted into the center comes out clean. Let the cake cool in the pan for 10 minutes, then place on a serving plate. *Makes 10–12 servings.*

German Sweet Chocolate Cake

The German Sweet Chocolate Cake was known as the "rich people's cake" because of the expensive ingredients required to make it.

*4 ounces semisweet baking
    chocolate, cut into pieces*
¼ cup water
2 cups sugar
*1 cup (2 sticks) unsalted
    butter, softened*

*4 large eggs, at room
    temperature*
3 cups all-purpose flour, sifted
1 teaspoon baking soda
1 cup buttermilk
1 ½ teaspoons vanilla extract

Preheat oven to 350° F. Place chocolate and water in a small saucepan, and heat over low heat until the chocolate is melted; cool.

In a large mixing bowl, beat the sugar and butter with an electric mixer until light and fluffy. Add the eggs one at a time, beating well after each addition. Stir in the chocolate mixture. Gradually add the flour, baking soda, buttermilk, and vanilla. Blend with the mixer at low speed until combined. Pour batter into three 9-inch nonstick round cake pans. Bake for 30 to 40 minutes, or until a toothpick inserted into the center comes out clean. Cool for 5 minutes and then remove the cakes from the pans.

To decorate, spread frosting between each cake layer and on top, leaving sides unfrosted. *Serves 12.*

Frosting

1 cup sugar

1 cup evaporated milk

½ cup (1 stick) salted butter

3 large egg yolks, slightly
   beaten at room temperature

1 ½ cups flaked coconut

1 ¼ cups chopped pecans

1 teaspoon vanilla extract

Place the sugar, milk, butter, and egg yolks in a medium saucepan. Cook over medium heat stirring constantly, until the mixture starts to bubble. Gradually stir in the coconut, pecans, and vanilla. Allow frosting to cool to room temperature before spreading onto the cake. *Makes about 2½* cups.

Gold Cake

The Gold Cake was originally called the Economical Gold Cake. The "economical" part began to be left off because the cake was often served at fancy gatherings such as graduation parties, weddings, and family reunions.

2 cups all-purpose flour, sifted
2 teaspoons baking powder
½ cup (1 stick) unsalted butter, softened
1 cup granulated sugar
3 large egg yolks, beaten at room temperature, plus 4 drops yellow food coloring

1 cup heavy cream
1 teaspoon vanilla extract
1 teaspoon powdered sugar
1 teaspoon cocoa powder

Preheat oven to 350° F. Sift the flour and baking powder together in a medium mixing bowl.

In a separate mixing bowl, cream the butter and sugar together with an electric mixer until fluffy. Add the egg yolks. Add the flour mixture and heavy cream gradually, alternating between the two, and mix at low speed. Fold in the vanilla. Continue to mix until batter is smooth.

Pour the batter into an 8 × 8 × 2-inch nonstick pan.

Bake for 50 minutes, or until a toothpick inserted into the center comes out clean. Let the cake cool for 5 minutes, then put it on a serving platter.

To decorate, combine powdered sugar and cocoa powder together. Place the cake on a serving plate and sprinkle cocoa mixture on the top and sides of the cake. *Serves 8.*

Lemon Jelly Cake

This cake is also known as the Sunshine Cake because its sweet lemony flavor always makes one burst into a big sunshine smile.

2 cups (4 sticks) unsalted butter, softened

2 ½ cups sugar

6 large eggs, at room temperature

½ cup fresh lemon juice

3 cups all-purpose flour, sifted

2 teaspoons baking powder

½ cup milk

2 tablespoons freshly grated lemon zest

Preheat oven to 325° F. Cream the butter and sugar together in a medium mixing bowl with an electric mixer. Add the eggs one at time, mixing well after each; then add the lemon juice. Gradually add the flour and baking powder to butter mixture, and mix on medium speed. Add the milk and lemon zest, continuing to mix until well blended.

Pour into a 10-inch nonstick Bundt pan. Bake for 90 minutes or until a toothpick inserted into the center comes out clean. Let the cake cool for 10 minutes before removing from pan to decorate. *Serves 12.*

Topping

1 ½ cups lemon preserves

1 tablespoon freshly grated lemon zest

To decorate, heat lemon preserves and lemon zest in a small saucepan until melted. Remove from the heat and drizzle over the top and sides of the cake. *Makes about 1½ cups.*

Moonshine Whiskey Cake

Because of the expense of commercially manufactured alcohol, moonshine (which is an illegally distilled whiskey made from corn mash) was served as a substitute on social occasions. It was also a great ingredient for desserts, including the Moonshine Whiskey Cake.

1 ½ cups (3 sticks) unsalted
    butter, softened
2 cups sugar
6 large eggs, at room
    temperature
½ cup dark molasses
3 ½ cups all-purpose flour
2 teaspoons baking powder

1 teaspoon ground nutmeg
1 teaspoon ground cloves
1 cup dark raisins
1 cup golden raisins
1 cup chopped candied pineapple
1 cup chopped candied cherries
3 cups chopped pecans
1 ½ cups bourbon

Preheat oven to 250° F. Cream the butter and sugar in a large mixing bowl with an electric mixer until fluffy. Add the eggs one at a time, beating well after each addition; add the molasses and mix well. In a separate large bowl, sift the flour, baking powder, nutmeg, and cloves together. Gradually add the flour mixture to the creamed butter and sugar, then stir in the fruit and nuts and the bourbon, alternating between the two.

Spoon batter into 2 non-stick 9 × 5-inch loaf pans and bake for 3½ hours or until a toothpick inserted into the center comes out clean. Remove the cakes from oven and let them cool for 10 minutes. Remove the cakes from the pans and wrap them with cheesecloth dampened with bourbon. Place them in a tin container and let sit until cakes have ripened for at least one month. *Serves 10–12.*

Mᴏʀɴɪɴɢ Cᴏffee Cᴀke

When this cake was made, there were hardly ever leftovers, but when there were they were used as an ingredient to make great bread pudding (*see* page 94).

1 ½ cups sugar
1 cup (2 sticks) unsalted butter
1 ½ cups heavy cream

3 cups all-purpose flour
3 ½ teaspoons baking powder
5 egg whites, stiffly beaten

Preheat oven to 350° F. Cream the butter and sugar in a large mixing bowl with an electric mixer until fluffy. Add the cream and the flour and baking powder to the butter and sugar, alternating between the two. Fold in the egg whites.

Pour the batter into a nonstick 12-inch baking pan and cover it with the topping. Bake at 350° F. for 60 minutes. Remove the cake from the oven and let it cool for 10 minutes. Cut the cake into squares (do not remove it from the pan) and serve. *Makes 10–12 servings.*

Topping

1 ½ cups chopped pecans
1 cup dark brown sugar
2 tablespoons ground cinnamon

½ cup all-purpose flour
1 cup (2 sticks) salted butter

Combine the pecans, sugar, cinnamon, flour, and butter in a large bowl and mix until it has a texture similar to cake crumbs. Spread over the top of the cake batter.

Old-Fashioned Pound Cake

One of the earliest pound cake recipes appeared in the 1794–1817 account book of a furniture maker from the state of Pennsylvania. Two hundred years later, the pound cake is still one of America's all-time favorite desserts—especially on a soul food dinner menu.

2 cups (4 sticks) unsalted
   butter, softened
3 cups sugar
8 large eggs, at room
   temperature

1 tablespoon vanilla extract
1 cup heavy cream
3 cups all-purpose flour, sifted
1 teaspoon baking soda
½ teaspoon salt

Preheat oven to 300° F. Cream the butter and sugar in a large mixing bowl with an electric mixer. Beat the eggs into the butter and sugar one at a time. Combine the vanilla and cream and mix the flour, baking soda, and salt together. Add the vanilla and cream mixture and the flour, baking soda, and salt mixture to the creamed mixture, alternating between the two.

Pour the batter into a 10-inch nonstick tube pan. Bake for 90 minutes or until a toothpick inserted into the center comes out clean. Remove the cake from the oven and let cool for 15 minutes. *Makes 10–12 servings.*

Buttermilk Pound Cake

For the ultimate orange flavor, sprinkle a tablespoon of Grand Marnier on top of the cake while it is still warm from the oven.

3 cups all-purpose flour

1 teaspoon baking soda

1 cup (2 sticks) unsalted butter, softened

2 ½ cups granulated sugar

5 large eggs, separated, at room temperature

1 ½ teaspoons freshly grated lemon zest

1 teaspoon almond extract

1 ½ cups buttermilk

1 teaspoon powdered sugar

Preheat oven to 350° F. Sift the flour and baking soda together in a medium mixing bowl and set aside. In a separate medium mixing bowl, cream the butter and sugar with an electric mixer until fluffy. Beat in the egg yolks one at a time until combined — *do not overbeat*. Add the lemon zest and almond extract. Beat the flour mixture and buttermilk into the creamed mixture, alternating between the two. In a separate small bowl, beat the egg whites until light but not dry and fold them into the batter.

Pour batter into a 10-inch nonstick tube pan. Bake for 90 minutes or until a toothpick inserted into the center comes out clean. Remove the cake from the oven and let cool for 10 minutes. Once cool, sprinkle with powdered sugar. *Serves 10–12.*

Strawberry Shortcake

If fresh strawberries are not available, use frozen strawberries (thawed and drained) as a substitute.

2 cups all-purpose flour

2 ½ teaspoons baking powder

½ cup granulated sugar

½ cup (1 stick) unsalted butter, chilled

½ cup heavy cream

2 large eggs, slightly beaten at room temperature

3 ½ cups fresh strawberries, halved

1 cup whipping cream

½ teaspoon light brown sugar

Preheat oven to 375° F. Place the flour, baking powder, and sugar in a medium mixing bowl. Using an electric mixer, slowly add the butter until the mixture becomes coarse. Slowly add the cream and eggs.

Spoon batter into a 9-inch nonstick round cake pan. Bake for 30 minutes or until a toothpick inserted into the center comes out clean. Remove the shortbread from the oven and let cool for 5 minutes before placing on a serving platter.

To decorate, refrigerate the strawberry halves for ½ hour. Beat the whipping cream with a wire whisk in a small bowl until soft peaks form. Layer the strawberry halves on top of the shortbread then spread the whip cream on top of the strawberries. Sprinkle with brown sugar. *Serves 6–8.*

Sweet Potato Cake

For the ultimate dessert, serve this cake with homemade Vanilla Ice Cream (*see* page 116).

1 cup (2 sticks) unsalted
   butter, softened
2 ½ cups sugar
5 large eggs, at room
   temperature
2 cups cooked sweet potatoes,
   mashed

3 cups all-purpose flour, sifted
2 teaspoons baking powder
1 teaspoon ground cinnamon
1 teaspoon ground nutmeg
1 cup heavy cream

Preheat oven to 350° F. Cream the butter and sugar in a large mixing bowl with an electric mixer until fluffy. Add the eggs, one at a time, mixing well after each addition. Blend in the sweet potatoes until smooth. In a separate medium bowl, sift together the dry ingredients and gradually stir them into the creamed mixture, alternating with the heavy cream. Pour batter into a 10-inch nonstick tube pan. Bake for 90 minutes or until a toothpick inserted into the center comes out clean. Remove from the oven and let cool for 5 minutes before removing from pan. *Serves 10–12.*

White Fruit Cake

If there are no raspberries and blueberries available, cherries and blackberries can be substituted.

1 cup (2 sticks) unsalted
  butter, softened
2 cups granulated sugar
½ teaspoon salt
3 cups all-purpose flour, sifted
3 teaspoons baking powder
1 cup milk

¼ cup raspberries, fresh or
  frozen
¼ cup blueberries, fresh or
  frozen
6 egg whites, at room
  temperature
1 ½ teaspoons powdered sugar

Preheat oven to 350° F. Cream the butter and sugar together in a large mixing bowl with an electric mixer until fluffy. In a separate medium mixing bowl, sift the salt, flour, and baking powder. Add the flour mixture to the creamed mixture, alternating with milk. Spoon in the raspberries and blueberries—*being careful not to crush the fruit.* Fold in the egg whites.

Pour the batter into a 10-inch nonstick Bundt pan. Bake for 90 minutes or until a toothpick inserted into the center comes out clean. Remove the cake from the oven and let cool for 10 minutes. Sprinkle with powdered sugar. *Serves 10–12.*

Orange Cake

For a richer flavor, sprinkle 2 tablespoons of dark rum into the icing.

2 cups sugar
1 cup (2 sticks) unsalted
  butter, softened
2 large eggs, at room
  temperature

¼ cup orange zest
½ cup heavy cream
2 ½ cups all-purpose flour, sifted
1 ½ teaspoons baking soda

Preheat oven to 350° F. Combine the sugar and butter in a large mixing bowl and mix with an electric mixer until fluffy. Add the eggs, zest, and cream. Sift the flour and baking soda together and add to the mixture. Beat with the mixer on low speed until the batter is smooth.

Pour batter into a 9 × 5-inch nonstick loaf pan. Bake for 40 minutes or until a toothpick inserted into the center comes out clean. Remove the cake from the oven and let cool for 10 minutes before removing it from the pan. *Serves 8–10.*

Icing

½ cup fresh orange juice
1 tablespoon orange zest

1 cup granulated sugar

Place orange juice, orange zest, and sugar into a small saucepan and bring to a boil over high heat. Pour over the cake while still warm. *Makes about 1⅓ cups.*

Yellow Cake

Before the availability of boxed cake mixes, this quick, easy, and inexpensive cake was frequently used.

1 cup vegetable shortening
2 ½ cups granulated sugar
4 large eggs, at room
    temperature
3 cups all-purpose flour, sifted
½ teaspoon salt

1 teaspoon baking soda
1 cup buttermilk
1 teaspoon vanilla extract
3 drops yellow food coloring
1 tablespoon powdered sugar

Preheat oven to 350° F. Place the shortening and sugar in a large mixing bowl. Mix with an electric mixer until fluffy. In a separate bowl, mix the flour, salt, and baking soda. Add the eggs, alternating with the flour mixture. Add the buttermilk and vanilla and continue mixing until batter is smooth. Mix in the food coloring.

Pour the batter into a 12 × 9-inch nonstick baking pan. Bake for 45 minutes or until a toothpick inserted into the center comes out clean. Remove the cake from the oven and let cool for 5 minutes.

Place the cooled cake on a serving plate and sprinkle the top and sides with powdered sugar. *Serves 10–12.*

Cookies,
Cookies,
Cookies

By definition, cookies are small cakes. They can be prepared crisp or soft, thick or thin, dark or light, plain or full of fruit and nuts. There are five basic types:

Rolled   A firm dough that is chilled, rolled thin, and cut out.

Drop   A firm dough that is dropped from a teaspoon.

Icebox   A fairly firm dough that is chilled thoroughly in the refrigerator and sliced thin.

Pressed   A moderately soft dough that is put through a cookie press to form well-defined shapes.

Bars   A dough that is baked in a pan and cut into bars after baking.

Apple-Nut Cookies

Not only are these cookies delicious, they can be used to make a great ice cream topping. Once the cookies have been baked, transfer them to a cool surface and leave them exposed to the air for about 2 hours. Crush the cookies into crumbs with your hands. Store the crumbs in an airtight container and refrigerate until ready to use.

1 cup (2 sticks) unsalted butter, softened

1 cup light brown sugar, firmly packed

1 large egg, at room temperature

1 ½ cups all-purpose flour, sifted

1 ½ teaspoons baking powder

1 teaspoon ground cinnamon

1 cup regular oats, uncooked

½ cup dark raisins

1 cup diced apple, peeled and cored

½ cup pecans, chopped

Preheat oven to 300° F. Cream the butter and sugar in a medium mixing bowl with an electric mixer until fluffy. Beat in the egg. In a separate bowl, combine the flour, baking powder, cinnamon, and oats. Gradually add the flour mixture to the butter and sugar mixture. Mix for 2 minutes on medium speed. Stir in raisins, apple, and pecans. Drop the dough by rounded tablespoonfuls, spaced 1½ inches apart, onto nonstick cookie sheets. Bake for 20 minutes or until the cookies turn slightly brown along the edges. Transfer them immediately to a cool, flat surface with a spatula. *Makes about 3 dozen.*

Butter Cookies

Butter Cookies are one of the most popular recipes in African-American homes. Almost as soon as they are made they disappear.

1 cup (2 sticks) salted butter,
    softened
½ cup sugar

1 ½ cups all-purpose flour, sifted
1 large egg, slightly beaten at
    room temperature

Preheat oven to 350° F. Place the butter and sugar in a medium mixing bowl and, using a hand mixer, beat the butter and sugar on medium speed for one minute. Add the flour and the egg and blend until the dough is soft—about 1½ minutes. Drop the dough by teaspoonfuls, spaced 1½ inches apart, onto nonstick cookie sheets and bake for 20 minutes or until the cookies are lightly golden. *Makes 2½ dozen.*

Butterscotch Cookies

These Butterscotch Cookies can be decorated by sprinkling some sifted powered sugar on top while they are still warm.

2 cups light brown sugar, firmly packed

3 cups all-purpose flour

2 ½ teaspoons baking powder

½ cup (1 stick) salted butter, melted

2 large eggs, beaten at room temperature

Combine the sugar, flour, and baking powder in a large mixing bowl. Add the melted butter and eggs and mix with a hand mixer for 2 minutes on low speed. Scoop the mixture onto a lightly floured board and knead. Shape the dough into one-inch rolls and wrap them with wax paper. Refrigerate the rolls for 12 hours.

Preheat oven to 350° F. Slice the rolls into about ¼-inch thick cookies and place 1½ inches apart on nonstick cookie sheets. Bake them for 12–15 minutes, or until the cookies turn golden brown. *Makes 4 dozen.*

Cashew and Coconut Cookies

This cookie dough can be stored in the freezer for up to a month before using it. Just be sure to place the dough in an airtight container before freezing it.

2 cups all-purpose flour, sifted

1 teaspoon baking powder

1 cup (2 sticks) unsalted
   butter, softened

½ cup powdered sugar

½ cup coconut flakes

½ cup chopped roasted and
   salted cashews

Preheat oven to 350° F. Sift the flour and baking powder together in a medium size mixing bowl. In a separate large mixing bowl, cream the butter and sugar until smooth with an electric mixer. Stir in the flour mixture, coconut, and cashews. Cover the dough with plastic wrap and refrigerate it for 1 hour.

Remove the dough from the refrigerator and roll it on a lightly floured surface to the thickness of ¼-inch. Cut it into 2-inch squares. Place the squares, spaced 1½ inches apart, onto nonstick cookie sheets.

Bake for 12 minutes or until the cookies turn golden brown. *Makes about 3 dozen.*

Chocolate Chip Cookies

An equivalent amount of semisweet chocolate chips can be substituted for the pecans in this Chocolate Chip Cookie recipe.

2 ½ cups all-purpose flour
1 teaspoon baking soda
1 teaspoon light brown sugar, firmly packed
1 cup (2 sticks) salted butter, softened

2 large eggs, at room temperature
1 ½ teaspoons vanilla extract
2 cups semi-sweet chocolate chips
¼ cup pecans, chopped

Preheat oven to 325° F. Sift the flour and baking soda together in a medium mixing bowl and set aside. In a separate large mixing bowl, mix the sugar and butter together with an electric mixer until it has a grainy texture. Add the eggs and vanilla to the butter and sugar mixture. Gradually add the flour mixture, chocolate chips, and nuts and mix until combined. *Be careful not to overmix.* Drop the dough by rounded tablespoonfuls, spaced 1½ inches apart, onto nonstick cookie sheets. Bake for about 20 minutes or until the cookies are golden brown. *Makes about 2½ dozen.*

Chocolate Mint Cookies

These cookies are best when served chilled—the mint flavor tastes more authentic—so place them in the refrigerator for 30 minutes before serving.

2 ½ cups all-purpose flour
½ teaspoon baking soda
¼ cup unsweetened cocoa powder
1 cup dark brown sugar, firmly
   packed
½ cup granulated sugar

1 cup (2 sticks) unsalted
   butter, softened
3 large eggs, at room
   temperature
1 ½ teaspoons pure mint extract
1 ½ cups mint chocolate chips

Preheat oven to 325° F. Using a wire whisk, mix the flour, baking soda, and cocoa powder together well in a medium mixing bowl. In a separate large mixing bowl, mix the sugars and butter with an electric mixer until it has the texture of grainy paste. Add the eggs and mint extract. Continue to mix until the paste becomes light and fluffy. Stir in the flour mixture and chocolate chips until combined. *Be careful not to overmix.*

Drop the dough by rounded tablespoonfuls, spaced 1½ inches apart, onto nonstick cookie sheets. Bake for 20 minutes.

Remove the cookies from the oven and place them on a cool surface. *Makes about 2½ dozen.*

Chocolate Pinwheels

Cookie cutters work well with this two-tone cookie. Once the dough has been sliced into ⅛-inch circles with a knife, cut with a cookie cutter.

1 ½ cups all-purpose flour, sifted
1 teaspoon baking powder
¼ teaspoon salt
½ cup (1 stick) unsalted butter, softened

½ cup sugar
1 large egg yolk, well beaten at room temperature
¼ cup heavy cream
½ cup unsweetened chocolate

Sift the flour, baking powder, and salt together in a medium mixing bowl. In a separate medium mixing bowl, cream the butter and sugar with an electric mixer until light and fluffy. Add the egg yolk. Add the flour mixture, alternating with the cream and beating after each addition until smooth. Divide the dough into two equal parts. Melt the chocolate in a double boiler and pour it on one of the halves of dough. Chill both rolls of dough for 1 hour.

Roll each half on a lightly floured board into a rectangular sheet about ⅛-inch thick). Placing the chocolate sheet on top of the plain sheet, roll them up together like a jelly roll. Chill the roll for 12 hours.

Preheat oven to 400° F. Cut the dough into ⅛-inch thick slices and place them, spaced 1½ inches apart on nonstick cookie sheets. Bake for 6 minutes. *Makes 3½ dozen.*

Coconut Crisp Cookies

This recipe doesn't call for sesame seeds, but adding about a tablespoon to the dough makes a very attractive batch of cookies.

½ cup (1 stick) unsalted butter, softened

½ cup granulated sugar

½ cup light brown sugar, firmly packed

1 large egg, at room temperature

1 ½ teaspoons vanilla extract

1 cup all-purpose flour, sifted

1 teaspoon baking powder

½ teaspoon baking soda

½ teaspoon salt

¼ teaspoon ground cinnamon

1 cup oatmeal, uncooked

1 cup coconut flakes

Preheat oven to 325° F. Using an electric mixer, mix the butter and sugars in a medium mixing bowl until the texture is grainy and pasty. Add the egg and vanilla. Continue to beat until light and fluffy. In a separate medium mixing bowl, sift together flour, baking powder, soda, salt, and cinnamon; add to the creamed butter and sugar mixture. Stir in the oatmeal and coconut. Drop by the teaspoonful, spaced 1½ inches apart, onto nonstick cookie sheets. Bake for 10 minutes or until the cookies are golden brown. *Makes 3½ dozen.*

Double Chocolate Chip Cookies

If no bourbon is available, dark rum can be used as a substitute.

2 ½ cups all-purpose flour
1 teaspoon baking soda
¼ cup cocoa powder
1¼ cups dark brown sugar,
   firmly packed
½ cup sugar

1 cup (2 sticks) salted butter,
   softened
3 large eggs, room temperature
1 tablespoon bourbon
2 cups semi-sweet chocolate
   chips

Preheat oven to 325° F. Mix the flour, baking soda, and cocoa together with a wire whisk in a medium mixing bowl. In a large mixing bowl, mix the sugars and butter together with an electric mixer until the texture is grainy and pasty. Beat in the eggs and bourbon. Gradually add the flour mixture and chocolate chips to the sugar mixture and mix until combined. *Do not overmix.*

Drop the dough by rounded tablespoons, spaced about 1½ inches apart, onto nonstick cookie sheets. Bake for 15 minutes. *Makes 3½ dozen.*

Drop Cookies

Drop cookies got their name from the way the cookies are made. Instead of rolling the cookie dough into small balls, the dough was scooped up with a teaspoon or tablespoon and dropped onto a baking sheet.

½ cup (1 stick) unsalted butter, softened

1 cup sugar

2 large eggs, well beaten at room temperature

2 cups all-purpose flour, sifted

1 ½ teaspoons baking powder

½ cup heavy cream

1 cup unsalted mixed nuts, chopped

Preheat oven to 375° F. In a medium mixing bowl, cream the butter and sugar with an electric mixer on medium speed until light and fluffy. Add the eggs. Adjust the mixer to low speed and gradually add the flour and baking powder, alternating with the cream, and beat until smooth. Fold in the nuts.

Drop the dough by rounded tablespoonfuls, spaced 1½ inches apart, onto nonstick cookie sheets. Bake for 10 minutes. *Makes 3½ dozen.*

Eggnog Cookies

Eggnog cookies were often prepared during Christmas and New Year. To add holiday colors, divide the dough into three equal batches and add red, green, or orange food coloring to each separate batch of dough before baking.

2 ½ cups all-purpose flour
1 ½ teaspoons baking powder
½ teaspoon ground nutmeg
½ teaspoon ground cinnamon
¼ teaspoon ground cloves
1 cup sugar
½ cup (1 stick) unsalted butter, softened

½ cup eggnog
3 large egg yolks, slightly beaten at room temperature
1 tablespoon ground nutmeg (for topping)
1 ½ teaspoons ground cinnamon (for topping)

Preheat oven to 325° F. Mix the flour, baking powder, nutmeg, cinnamon, and cloves together in a medium mixing bowl with a wire whisk. In a separate medium mixing bowl, cream the sugar and butter with a hand mixer until the texture is grainy and pasty. Add the eggnog and egg yolks and continue to mix until smooth. Gradually add the flour mixture, mixing on low speed until the dough is combined. Drop the dough by rounded teaspoonfuls, spaced 1 inch apart, onto nonstick cookie sheets. Sprinkle lightly with nutmeg and cinnamon. Bake for 20 minutes or until the edges turn light brown. *Makes 3 dozen.*

Gingersnaps

For a stronger ginger flavor, add about ½ teaspoon freshly ground ginger to the recipe. This will send Gingersnaps lovers over the top.

2 ½ cups all-purpose flour
1 tablespoon ground ginger
½ teaspoon ground cloves
½ teaspoon ground cinnamon
½ teaspoon baking soda
½ teaspoon ground black pepper
1 ½ cups dark brown sugar,
  firmly packed

1 cup (2 sticks) salted butter,
  softened
1 large egg, at room
  temperature
¼ cup dark molasses

Combine the flour, ginger, cloves, cinnamon, baking soda, and black pepper together in a medium mixing bowl and mix well with a wire whisk. In a separate large mixing bowl, mix the sugar and butter with an electric mixer on medium speed until blended. Add the egg and molasses and beat until light and fluffy. Add the flour mixture slowly to the molasses mixture. Cover the dough with plastic wrap and refrigerate for 1 hour.

Preheat oven to 325° F. Roll 1-inch balls of dough and place on a nonstick cookie sheet, spacing the balls 1½ inches apart. Bake for 20 minutes. *Makes about 3 dozen.*

Ginger Tea Cookies

These ginger tea cookies make a great holiday open-house party favorite. You may want to double the recipe ingredients so that lots of cookies will be available.

2 cups all-purpose flour
1 teaspoon cream of tartar
1 teaspoon baking soda
2 teaspoons ground ginger
1 teaspoon diced crystallized ginger
¼ teaspoon ground cloves

½ teaspoon salt
¾ cup (1½ sticks) salted butter, softened
1 cup sugar
2 large eggs, at room temperature
1 teaspoon vanilla extract

Combine the flour, tartar, baking soda, ground ginger, crystallized ginger, cloves, and salt together in a medium mixing bowl and mix well with a wire whisk. In a separate large mixing bowl, beat the butter and sugar with an electric mixer until fluffy. Add the eggs and vanilla. Gradually add the flour mixture and mix on low speed until combined. Cover the dough with plastic wrap and refrigerate for 1 hour.

Preheat the oven to 325° F. Form the dough into 1-inch balls and place them onto nonstick cookie sheets, spacing the balls about 1½ inches apart. Bake for 20 minutes. *Makes 4 dozen.*

Lemon Cookies

For a deeper yellow color, add 3 drops of yellow food coloring to the cookie dough before rolling it out and baking.

¾ cup (1½ sticks) unsalted
  butter, softened
1 cup sugar
1 large egg yolk

⅓ cup fresh lemon juice
2 teaspoons grated lemon zest
2 cups all-purpose flour, sifted
¼ teaspoon salt

Preheat oven to 375° F. Combine the butter and sugar, mixing them with an electric mixer until fluffy. Add the egg yolk, lemon juice, and lemon zest, then fold in the flour and salt. Drop the dough by tablespoonfuls, spaced about 1½ inches apart, onto non-stick cookie sheets. Bake for 10 minutes. *Makes about 2 dozen.*

Lemon Squares

These lemon squares taste best when served chilled. Place them in the refrigerator until ready to serve.

Crust

2 cups all-purpose flour, sifted

½ cup powdered sugar

1 cup (2 sticks) salted butter, softened

Filling

4 large eggs, slightly beaten at room temperature

1 ½ cups sugar

½ cup all-purpose flour

1 ½ teaspoons baking powder

¼ cup fresh lemon juice

Preheat oven to 325° F. In a large mixing bowl, combine the crust ingredients and mix with an electric mixer at low speed until mixture starts to crumble. Press the mixture evenly in the bottom of a nonstick 13 × 9-inch pan. Bake the crust for 30 minutes or until light golden brown. Remove the crust from the oven and set it aside.

In a large mixing bowl combine the filling ingredients, except the lemon juice, and blend well with an electric mixer. Stir in the lemon juice.

Pour the filling in the crust. Bake for 30 minutes or until top is light golden brown. Remove from the oven and cool.

Spread the frosting over the cooked lemon filling. Cut the lemon square into small bars. *Makes about 3 dozen.*

Frosting

1 cup powdered sugar

¼ cup fresh lemon juice

Place the powdered sugar and lemon juice in a small bowl and blend with an electric mixer on medium speed until smooth.

Mama's Tea Cakes

Tea Cakes were always used to measure how well one could bake. If your Tea Cakes passed the test of neighbors your reputation as a cook would be made. This recipe is dedicated to my mother and grandmother, who were great food lovers.

1 ½ cups sugar
1 cup vegetable shortening
2 large eggs, at room
temperature

2 teaspoons baking powder
1 tablespoon vanilla extract
2 tablespoons whipping cream
3 ½ cups all-purpose flour

Preheat oven to 325° F. Place the sugar and vegetable shortening in a large mixing bowl. Cream with an electric mixer until light and fluffy. Add the eggs one at time, mixing after each addition. Add the baking powder, vanilla, cream, and flour and mix well.

Roll the dough into 1-inch balls and, spacing them 1½ inches apart, place them on nonstick cookie sheets. Flatten each ball with your fingers or a nonstick spatula. Bake for 10 minutes or until they turn golden brown. *Makes 4 dozen.*

Molasses Cookies

Molasses Cookies are known as poor man's cookies because they can be made with ingredients that are cheap and can be found in almost anybody's kitchen.

⅓ cup vegetable shortening
¼ cup sugar
1 large egg, at room
   temperature
½ teaspoon ground cinnamon

½ teaspoon ground ginger
2 teaspoons baking powder
2 cups all-purpose flour
¼ cup heavy cream
1 cup dark molasses

Preheat oven to 350° F. In a medium mixing bowl, cream the shortening and sugar with an electric mixer. Add the egg. Sift all the dry ingredients together and then add to the shortening mixture. Mix it until the texture is crumbly. Mix the cream and molasses together and add them to the shortening mixture.

Drop the dough by teaspoonfuls, spacing them 1½ inches apart, onto nonstick cookie sheets. Bake for 10 minutes. *Makes 4 dozen.*

PUMPKIN COOKIES

If cooked pumpkin is not available, cooked sweet potatoes can be substituted.

2 ¼ cups all-purpose flour
1 ½ teaspoons baking soda
  2 teaspoons pumpkin pie spice
1 ¼ cups dark brown sugar,
    firmly packed
  ¼ cup granulated sugar

1 cup salted butter, softened
1 large egg, at room
  temperature
1 cup cooked pumpkin, canned
  or fresh
2 teaspoons vanilla extract

Preheat oven to 325° F. Combine the flour, baking soda, and pumpkin pie spice in a medium mixing bowl and mix them well with a wire whisk. In a separate large mixing bowl, cream the sugars and butter with an electric mixer until the texture is grainy and pasty. Add the egg, pumpkin, and vanilla and continue to mix until the texture is smooth. Gradually fold in the flour mixture.

Drop the dough by rounded tablespoonfuls, spacing them 1½ inches apart, onto nonstick cookie sheets. Bake for 20 minutes. *Makes 2 dozen.*

Oatmeal and Raisin Cookies

Try substituting chopped pecans or chocolate chips for the raisins in this recipe.

1 cup sugar	½ teaspoon salt
½ cup vegetable shortening	1 ¼ teaspoons baking soda
1 large egg, room temperature	1 ½ teaspoons vanilla extract
¼ cup dark molasses	1 ¼ cups oatmeal, uncooked
2 cups all-purpose flour, sifted	½ cup dark raisins

Preheat oven to 350° F. Cream the sugar and shortening with an electric mixer in a medium mixing bowl. Add the egg and molasses and beat well. Combine the flour, salt, and baking soda and gradually add them to the cream mixture. Add the vanilla and then stir in the oatmeal and the raisins.

Drop the dough by rounded teaspoonfuls, spaced 1½ inches apart, onto nonstick cookie sheets. Bake for 15 minutes. *Makes 3½ dozen.*

Pecan Crisp Cookies

This traditional soul food recipe calls for pecans but macadamia nuts or hazelnuts can be used instead.

1 cup unsalted butter, softened	2 ½ cups all-purpose flour
2 ½ cups light brown sugar, firmly packed	¼ teaspoon salt
2 large eggs, well beaten at room temperature	½ teaspoon baking soda
	1 cup fresh pecans, chopped

Preheat oven to 350° F. Cream the butter and sugar in a medium mixing bowl with an electric mixer. Add the eggs, continuing to mix the dough until well combined. Add the flour, salt, and baking soda. Fold in the pecans.

Drop by rounded teaspoonfuls, spaced 1½ inches apart, onto nonstick cookie sheets. Bake for 12 minutes. *Makes about 3 dozen.*

Peanut Butter Cookies

These cookies are best when served warm. Serve them right out of the oven or quickly reheat them in the microwave (about 30 seconds for 4 cookies).

¾ cup peanut butter	1 large egg
¼ cup unsalted butter, softened	1 teaspoon vanilla extract
½ cup light brown sugar	1 ½ cups all purpose flour
½ cup granulated sugar	1 ½ teaspoons baking soda

Preheat oven to 350° F. Place the peanut butter, butter, and sugars in a medium mixing bowl and mix with an electric mixer until combined. Add the egg and vanilla. Sift the flour and baking soda together and gradually add them to the peanut butter mixture.

Drop the dough by tablespoonfuls, spaced 2 inches apart, onto nonstick cookie sheets and flatten out each cookie with a fork. Bake for 15 minutes. *Makes 2½ dozen.*

Raisin Cookies

Dried cherries and cranberries can be substituted for the dark and golden raisins.

1 cup salted butter, softened
1 ½ cups sugar
2 large eggs, well beaten at
   room temperature
2 teaspoons vanilla extract
3 cups all-purpose flour

1 teaspoon baking soda
1 ¼ teaspoons ground cinnamon
½ teaspoon ground allspice
1 cup dark raisins
½ cup golden raisins
1 cup pecans, chopped

Preheat oven to 375° F. Place the butter and sugar in a medium mixing bowl and cream them with an electric mixer until fluffy. Add the eggs and vanilla. Sift the flour, baking soda, cinnamon, and allspice together and add this to the butter mixture, continuing to mix until well combined. Stir in the raisins and pecans.

Drop tablespoonfuls onto nonstick cookie sheets about 2 inches apart. Bake for 12 minutes. *Makes 3½ dozen.*

Sugar Cookies

Colored sugar sprinkles can be purchased at the grocery store and sprinkled on the cookies as a decorative alternative to the granulated sugar called for in the recipe.

2 ½ cups all-purpose flour

1 teaspoon baking powder

1 teaspoon baking soda

1 ½ cups sugar

1 large egg, at room temperature

1 tablespoon vanilla extract

1 cup unsalted butter, softened

¼ cup sugar (for sprinkling)

Preheat oven to 325° F. Place flour, baking powder, and baking soda in a medium mixing bowl and mix with a wire whisk until well combined. In a separate large mixing bowl, cream the sugar, egg, vanilla, and butter with an electric mixer until fluffy. Add the flour mixture and blend for 2 minutes on slow speed.

Make balls with your hands using 2 teaspoons of dough for each one and space them 2 inches apart on nonstick cookie sheets. Sprinkle the top of each ball with sugar and bake for 20 minutes. *Makes about 4 dozen.*

Vanilla Nut Cookies

To enhance the liquor flavor of these cookies add 2 tablespoons of dark rum to the dough.

 1 cup unsalted butter, softened
1 ½ cups sugar
 2 large eggs, at room
    temperature
 1 tablespoon vanilla extract
 1 teaspoon vanilla seeds taken
    from the vanilla pod

 2 cups all-purpose flour
 1 teaspoon baking soda
 ¼ teaspoon salt
 1 cup walnuts, chopped

Preheat oven to 375° F. In a medium mixing bowl, cream the butter and sugar with an electric mixer until fluffy. Add the eggs, vanilla, and vanilla seeds. Sift the flour, baking soda, and salt together and slowly add to the butter mixture, mixing well. Stir in the walnuts.

Drop the dough by tablespoonfuls, spaced 1½ inches apart, onto nonstick cookie sheets. Bake for 10 minutes. *Makes 3 dozen.*

Pies, Pies, Pies

The key to a flaky, tasty pie crust is making a good pastry. A good baked pastry has a blistery, pebbly surface, which indicates it will be flaky when cut. It should be tender and easily cut with a fork, but not so tender that it crumbles. The crust should be fairly thin, so that the bottom as well as the rim will become crisp. The only ingredients required to make the best pie pastry are:

Flour   A good quality, all-purpose flour is best for pie pastry. Bread flour tends to make a heavier and tougher crust. Cake flour makes a tender crust that crumbles easily.

Vegetable Shortening   A firm shortening, such as hydrogenated vegetable fat, works best. Lard or butter may be used but they are more difficult to work with and seldom give a tender crust because they contain quite a bit of water and, in butter, milk solids.

Salt   Salt is necessary for flavor in the pie pastry because the other ingredients are bland. A slightly salty crust is pleasing when combined with any pie filling.

Wilbert's Perfect Pie Crust

This easy pie crust can be made in advance and frozen until you are ready to use it. It will keep for up to 3 months in the freezer.

1 cup all-purpose flour, sifted
¼ cup vegetable shortening

⅛ teaspoon salt

Place all the ingredients in a medium mixing bowl and mix on low speed with an electric mixer until lightly blended. Gently form the dough into a ball, then roll it out between sheets of wax paper into a 10-inch circle. Remove the wax paper, and fold the dough in half, and then in half again so that it forms a triangle with one curved side. Transfer the crust to a 9-inch pie pan. Unfold the dough and fit into the pie pan, trimming as necessary. Flute the crust decoratively or press the edges with a fork.

For a flakier crust, preheat the oven to 350° F. Prick the bottom and sides of the crust with a fork. Bake for 10 minutes then remove from the oven and let cool. *Makes one unbaked 9-inch single pie crust.*

Sweet Potato Pie

Sweet potato pie is one of the most popular soul food desserts. It is usually prepared for holidays and weekly Sunday dinners.

1 ½ cups cooked mashed sweet potatoes
1 tablespoon salted butter
½ cup sugar
4 large eggs, well beaten at room temperature
1 cup whipping cream

½ teaspoon ground cinnamon
¼ teaspoon ground nutmeg
¼ teaspoon ground mace
¼ teaspoon ground allspice
1 unbaked 9-inch pie shell (see recipe on page 65)

Preheat oven to 400° F. Combine all the ingredients in a large mixing bowl and, using an electric mixer, mix on medium speed until the texture is smooth, containing no lumps. Pour into a pie shell and bake for 15 minutes. Then lower the temperature to 350° F. and bake for an additional 30 minutes or until set. *Serves 8.*

Frozen Blueberry Jam Pie

Fresh raspberries can be used instead of blueberries to make this delicious pie.

2 cups graham cracker crumbs
½ cup walnuts, finely chopped
½ cup (1 stick) unsalted butter,
*   melted*
¼ cup honey
½ teaspoon ground cinnamon

2 ½ cups fresh blueberries, washed
*   and drained*
½ cup sugar
1 cup whipping cream
¼ cup cornstarch

Preheat oven to 350° F. Combine graham cracker crumbs, walnuts, butter, honey, and cinnamon in a medium mixing bowl and mix well with an electric mixer on low speed until combined. Press the cracker mix into a 9-inch pie pan and bake for 10 minutes. Remove the crust from the oven and set aside.

Press the blueberries through a sieve or food mill with ½ cup sugar and set aside. In a medium mixing bowl, whip the cream and cornstarch together with a wire whisk until the mixture holds its shape. Spoon the cream into the crust. Pour the blueberry mixture in a thin stream over the top to create a marbled effect. Freeze for at least 3 hours. Remove from the freezer, cut into 8 wedges, and serve. *Makes 8 servings.*

Delicious Peanut Pie

This tasty peanut pie is best served chilled. Place the pie in the refrigerator for at least one hour before serving.

1 cup light corn syrup
1 cup sugar
3 large eggs, well beaten at room temperature

1 cup chunky peanut butter
1 unbaked 9-inch pie shell (see recipe on page 65)

Preheat oven to 400° F. Blend the syrup, sugar, eggs, and peanut butter together with an electric mixer until combined, then pour the mixture into the pie crust. Bake for 15 minutes, then lower the temperature to 350° F. and bake for an additional 30 minutes or until the filling appears slightly less set in the center than around the edges. *Makes 8 servings.*

Southern Pecan Pie

To decorate this pie, take ¾ cup of pecan halves and place them on top of the pecan filling in a circular pattern before baking.

½ cup sugar

1 cup light corn syrup

3 large eggs, well beaten at room temperature

4 tablespoons salted butter, softened

1 tablespoon vanilla extract

1 ½ cups chopped pecans

1 unbaked 9-inch pie shell (see recipe on page 65)

Preheat oven to 425° F. Place the sugar and syrup in a small heavy saucepan and cook over low heat, stirring constantly until it becomes thick. Once it has thickened, gradually add the eggs, stirring quickly. Remove the mixture from the heat and add the butter, vanilla, and pecans.

Pour the mixture into pie crust. Bake for 10 minutes, then lower the temperature to 325° F. and bake for an additional 30 minutes. *Serves 8.*

Key Lime Pie

"Floribbean" is a cuisine combining the flavors of Florida with a Caribbean flair. The key lime pie is one of the oldest Floribbean recipes.

1 ½ cups graham cracker crumbs
½ cup sugar
½ cup unsalted butter
2 large eggs, room temperature
1 15-ounce can sweetened condensed milk

½ cup fresh lime juice
1 cup sour cream
½ cup sugar
¼ teaspoon salt
1 tablespoon lime zest

Preheat oven to 350° F. Combine the graham cracker crumbs, sugar, and butter in a medium mixing bowl and mix with an electric mixer until combined. Press the cracker mix into a 9-inch pie pan. Bake the crust for 10 minutes then remove it from the oven and set it aside.

Beat the eggs and milk together in a medium mixing bowl, then add the juice. Pour the filling into the pie crust and bake at 350° F. for 15 minutes or until set. After removing the pie, raise the oven temperature to 400° F. and allow it to preheat while making the topping.

In a separate medium mixing bowl, prepare the topping by combining the sour cream, sugar, and salt. Spread the sour cream mixture on top of the set filling. Bake for about 10 minutes to allow the topping to set. Remove the pie from the oven and let it cool. Garnish with lime zest. Refrigerate until ready to serve. *Serves 8.*

Butterscotch Meringue Pie

This delicious butterscotch meringue pie is best when served slightly frozen. Place the pie in the freezer for about 45 minutes or until it turns slightly stiff (check this by inserting a knife in the center) before serving.

½ cup all-purpose flour, sifted

1 cup light brown sugar

½ cup granulated sugar

¼ teaspoon salt

2 cups milk, scalded

4 egg yolks, slightly beaten at room temperature

3 tablespoons salted butter, softened

1 teaspoon vanilla extract

1 unbaked 9-inch pie shell (see recipe on page 65)

4 egg whites, at room temperature

¼ teaspoon cream of tartar

¼ teaspoon salt

Preheat oven to 350° F. Combine the flour, sugars, and salt in a small saucepan. Gradually add the milk while cooking over medium heat, stirring constantly until the mixture thickens and boils. Cook the mixture for 2 additional minutes, continuing to stir, then remove from heat. Add a small amount of the hot milk mixture to the egg yolks and stir well. Pour the egg yolk mix into the saucepan containing the remaining hot milk mixture. Cook for one minute over medium heat, stirring constantly. Stir in the butter and vanilla, then remove from the heat and allow to cool slightly. Pour the filling into the pie shell and cool.

For the meringue topping, combine egg whites, cream of tartar, and salt in a medium mixing bowl. Beat the mixture with an electric mixer until frothy. Gradually add the sugar and beat until stiff glossy peaks form. Spread on the top of the pie. Bake for 12 minutes or until meringue turns golden brown. *Serves 8.*

Apple Pie

To add a glaze to this apple pie, beat one large egg together with about ¼ teaspoon sugar, then take a pastry brush and coat the top and sides of the pie shell pastry with the egg wash before baking.

1 cup sugar

2 teaspoons ground cinnamon

½ teaspoon ground allspice

½ teaspoon ground nutmeg

1 tablespoon all-purpose flour

½ cup dark raisins

6 cups (about 4 large apples) cubed tart apples, peeled and cored

1 unbaked 9-inch pie shell (see recipe on page 65)

Crumb Topping

½ cup all-purpose flour

½ cup sugar

½ teaspoon ground allspice

¼ cup (½ stick) salted butter, chilled

Preheat oven to 375° F. In a large mixing bowl, stir together the sugar, cinnamon, allspice, nutmeg, and flour. Add the raisins and apples, tossing until the fruit is coated with the sugar mixture. Transfer the apple mixture into the pie shell.

For the crumb topping, place the flour, sugar, allspice, and butter in a medium mixing bowl and mix with your hands until it becomes crumbly. Sprinkle the topping over the pie, covering the filling completely. Bake for 25 minutes. Reduce the oven temperature to 350° F. and bake for an additional 25 minutes or until the top turns golden brown. *Serves 8.*

Georgia Peach Pie

This Peach Pie recipe was taken from my friends in Georgia, the Peach State, and defines what a Georgia Peach Pie should be.

1 cup granulated sugar

3 tablespoons all-purpose flour

1 teaspoon ground cloves

½ cup light corn syrup

3 large eggs, at room temperature

3 cups sliced fresh peaches, peeled

¼ cup salted butter, softened

1 unbaked 9-inch pie shell (see recipe on page 65)

¼ cup walnuts, coarsely chopped

¼ cup pecans, coarsely chopped

¼ cup all-purpose flour

¼ cup light brown sugar, firmly packed

3 tablespoons salted butter, softened

Preheat oven to 400° F. In a large mixing bowl, combine the granulated sugar, flour, cloves, corn syrup, and eggs and, using an electric mixer, beat on medium speed for one minute. Stir in the peaches and butter and spoon the filling into the pie shell.

For the topping, place the walnuts, pecans, flour, brown sugar, and butter in a small mixing bowl and mix well. Sprinkle the mixture on top of the peach filling. Bake for 40 minutes or until the center is set. *Makes 8 servings.*

Black Walnut Pie

This pie's flavor can be enhanced by adding a tablespoon of rum to the pie filling before baking.

½ cup granulated sugar

½ cup dark brown sugar

1 cup light corn syrup

¼ cup (½ stick) salted butter, softened

3 large eggs, slightly beaten at room temperature

1 ¼ cups walnuts, chopped

1 cup dark raisins

1 cup golden raisins

1 tablespoon granulated sugar

½ teaspoon ground cinnamon

1 tablespoon all-purpose flour

1 unbaked 9-inch pie shell (see recipe on page 65)

Preheat oven to 375° F. Combine the ½ cup granulated sugar, brown sugar, and corn syrup in a medium heavy saucepan and heat over medium heat until it starts to boil. Remove the saucepan from the heat and add the butter, stirring until it melts. Combine the eggs, walnuts, and raisins in a large mixing bowl, add the hot sugar mixture to it and set aside.

In a separate small mixing bowl, mix one tablespoon of granulated sugar, cinnamon, and flour and sprinkle on the bottom of the pie shell. Pour the walnut mixture on top. Bake for 40 minutes or until the filling is set. *Serves 8.*

Bourbon Pie

This bourbon pie can be prepared and kept in the refrigerator for up to one week before serving.

1 16-ounce (1 pound) box
chocolate-snap cookies,
crushed

½ cup (1 stick) unsalted butter,
melted

21 marshmallows

1 ½ cups evaporated milk

½ pint whipping cream

3 tablespoons bourbon

1 tablespoon chocolate-snap
cookie crumbs (for topping)

Preheat oven to 350° F. In a large mixing bowl, mix the crushed cookies and melted butter together. Pat the mixture into a 9-inch round pie pan and bake for 10 minutes or until the crust hardens. Remove it from the oven and set it aside to cool. In a medium heavy saucepan, melt the marshmallows and milk over low heat. Be careful not to let the mixture boil. Cool the milk and marshmallows completely and then add the whipping cream and bourbon.

Pour the filling into the cooled pie shell. Sprinkle cookie crumbs on top of the filling. Chill the pie in the refrigerator until ready to serve. *Serves 8.*

PUMPKIN PIE

Top this Pumpkin Pie with Cool Whip and sprinkle ground cinnamon on top.

2 cups cooked mashed pumpkin
½ cup honey
1 teaspoon ground cinnamon
½ teaspoon ground allspice
½ teaspoon ground ginger
½ teaspoon ground cloves

4 large eggs, slightly beaten at
    room temperature
1 ½ cups evaporated milk
1 unbaked 9-inch pie shell (see
    recipe on page 65)

Preheat oven to 400° F. In a large mixing bowl combine the pumpkin, honey, and spices and blend with an electric mixer on medium speed. Next, add the eggs and mix well. Adjust the mixer speed to low and gradually add the milk, continuing to mix until well blended.

Pour the pumpkin mixture into the pie shell and bake for 40 minutes or until a knife inserted into the center comes out clean. Remove the pie from the oven and allow it to cool completely. Store in the refrigerator until ready to serve. *Makes 8 servings.*

Icebox Pie

This pie is an old favorite because it can be put together quickly and doesn't require a crust.

6 *egg whites, at room*
   temperature
1 *cup sugar*
1 ½ *teaspoons vanilla extract*

1 *cup pecans, chopped*
1 *cup graham crackers,*
   crumbled
1 ½ *cups shredded coconut*

Preheat oven to 350° F. Place the egg whites in a medium mixing bowl and, using an electric mixer, beat until stiff peaks form. Fold in the sugar and vanilla. Gradually fold in the pecans, graham cracker crumbs, and coconut.

Pour mixture into a 9-inch nonstick pie pan. Bake for 30 minutes or until the filling is set. Remove the pie from the oven and let it cool. Chill in the refrigerator until ready to serve. *Makes 8 servings.*

Pinto Bean Pie

Cooked mashed lima beans or kidney beans can be substituted for pinto beans.

1 cup cooked pinto beans, mashed
½ cup pecans, chopped
½ cup shredded coconut
1 cup light brown sugar
2 large eggs, slightly beaten at room temperature

3 tablespoons salted butter, softened
1 teaspoon vanilla extract
½ cup evaporated milk
1 unbaked 9-inch pie shell (see recipe on page 65)

Preheat oven to 300° F. Combine beans, pecans, coconut, sugar, eggs, butter, vanilla and milk in a food processor and blend on low speed until smooth. *Be careful not to overmix.*

Pour the bean mixture into the pie shell and bake for 40 minutes or until the filling is set. *Makes 8 servings.*

Chess Pie

Serve this chess pie chilled. Place it in the refrigerator at least two hours before serving.

4 large eggs, at room
    temperature
1 ½ cups sugar
1 cup whipping cream
1 cup (2 sticks) butter, melted

1 tablespoon all-purpose flour
½ teaspoon ground nutmeg
1 unbaked 9-inch pie shell (see
    recipe on page 65)

Preheat oven to 300° F. Place the eggs and sugar in a large mixing bowl and mix with an electric mixer on medium speed until fluffy. Add the cream, butter, and flour to the egg mixture and beat together until light and fluffy. Stir in the nutmeg.

Pour the filling into the pie shell and bake for 1 hour or until the filling is set. *Makes 8 servings.*

Custard Pie

Serve this pie with fresh blueberries and sliced strawberries.

8 large eggs, at room
  temperature
1 cup milk
2 teaspoons vanilla extract
1 cup sugar

1 tablespoon all-purpose flour
1 cup (2 sticks) butter, melted
1 unbaked 9-inch pie shell (see
  recipe on page 65)

Preheat oven to 300° F. Place the eggs in a large mixing bowl and beat with an electric mixer on medium speed for two minutes. Add the milk, vanilla, sugar, flour, and butter and beat until light and fluffy.

Pour the filling into the pie shell and bake for 50 minutes or until the filling is set. *Serves 8.*

Strawberry Pie

his pie can be made up to 2 days before serving.

1 cup graham cracker crumbs
½ cup sugar
½ cup (1 stick) salted butter
4 tablespoons strawberry Jell-O
3 tablespoons cornstarch

1 cup water
1 cup sugar
1 pint fresh strawberries, halved
1½ cups Cool Whip

Preheat oven to 350° F. First, prepare the crust by combining the graham cracker crumbs, sugar, and butter in a medium mixing bowl and mixing with an electric mixer. Press the cracker mixture into a 9-inch pie pan and bake for 10 minutes. Remove the crust from the oven and set aside to cool.

In a small heavy saucepan, mix the Jell-O and cornstarch. Add the water and sugar. Bring the mixture to a boil over medium heat, stirring constantly. Remove from the heat and let it cool completely, then stir in the strawberries.

Pour the filling into cooled baked pie shell and spread it with Cool Whip evenly on top. Place the pie in the refrigerator at least 2 hours before serving. *Serves 8.*

Deep South Sugar Pie

Keep this pie in the refrigerator until ready to serve.

2 tablespoons unsalted butter, softened

1 tablespoon all-purpose flour

2 cups milk

1 ½ cups dark brown sugar

1 whole egg, plus 2 egg yolks, well beaten at room temperature

1 tablespoon vanilla extract

1 cup golden raisins

1 unbaked 9-inch pie shell (see recipe on page 65)

2 tablespoons granulated sugar

½ teaspoon salt

3 egg whites, stiffly beaten at room temperature

Preheat oven to 325° F. In a medium heavy saucepan combine the butter and flour and stir over low heat until smooth. Gradually add the milk, stirring constantly. Remove the mixture from the heat and add the brown sugar, stirring until it is dissolved. Stir in the beaten egg and yolks, then add the vanilla and raisins. Pour the mixture into the pie shell and bake for 60 minutes or until firm. Remove the pie and increase the oven temperature to 375° F.

For the meringue topping, lightly fold the sugar and salt into the stiffly beaten egg whites. Spoon the meringue onto the top of the baked pie. Bake for 20 minutes or until the meringue turns golden brown. *Serves 8.*

Although "Vinegar Pie" does not sound very appealing, its combination of sweet and tangy flavors is very tasty.

1 cup sugar	*1 tablespoon salted butter*
3 large eggs, at room temperature	*1 teaspoon lemon extract*
½ cup cider vinegar	*1 unbaked 9-inch pie shell (see recipe on page 65)*
2 tablespoons all-purpose flour	*1 ½ cups whipping cream*
1 cup water	*½ teaspoon ground cinnamon*

Combine the sugar, eggs, vinegar, flour, and water in a double boiler and cook on low heat until thick and smooth, stirring occasionally. Just before removing the mixture from the heat, stir in the butter and lemon extract. Pour the filling into the pie shell.

Cool the pie in the refrigerator for at least 3 hours. Before serving, mix the whipping cream with an electric mixer on medium speed for 2 minutes or until it turns thick and spreadable. Spread the whipped cream evenly on top of the pie and sprinkle with cinnamon. Keep in the refrigerator until ready to serve. *Serves 8.*

Buttermilk Pie

Keep this pie refrigerated until ready to serve.

1 ½ cups sugar

1 tablespoon all-purpose flour

3 large eggs, slightly beaten at room temperature

1 ¼ cups buttermilk

½ cup (1 stick) salted butter

2 teaspoons vanilla extract

1 unbaked 9-inch pie shell (see recipe on page 65)

Preheat oven to 350° F. Combine the sugar, flour, eggs, buttermilk, and butter in a medium mixing bowl and, using an electric mixer, mix on low speed until smooth. Blend in the vanilla. Pour the filling into the pie shell and bake for 50 minutes or until the filling is set. *Makes 8 servings.*

Rum Pie

If desired, add ½ cup dark raisins to this pie before baking. The raisins will absorb the rum and create a great flavor.

3 egg yolks, at room
   temperature
1 cup sugar
⅓ cup unflavored gelatin
¼ cup cold water
1 cup whipping cream

¼ cup dark rum
1 unbaked 9-inch pie shell (see
   recipe on page 65)
1 teaspoon unsweetened cocoa
   (for topping)

In a medium mixing bowl, beat the yolks with an electric mixer on low speed until light. Blend in the sugar. Place the gelatin and water in a small heavy saucepan. Bring to a boil over low heat then pour over the sugar and egg mixture, stirring briskly with a whisk. Whisk the whipping cream until it becomes firm and stiff. Fold the whipping cream into the egg mixture and add the rum. Allow the mixture to cool until it begins to set, then pour it into the pie shell. Sprinkle the top with cocoa. Refrigerate for 2 hours before serving. *Makes 8 servings.*

Chocolate Pie

To add even more chocolate flavor to this pie, use ¼ cup semi-sweet chocolate chips in addition to the cocoa when making the filling.

1 ½ cups graham cracker crumbs
½ cup sugar
½ cup unsalted butter
1 cup milk
2 egg yolks, well beaten at room temperature
2 tablespoons cornstarch
1 ½ teaspoons vanilla extract

1 cup sugar
¼ cup unsweetened cocoa
3 egg whites, at room temperature
¼ teaspoon salt
¼ cup sugar
1 teaspoon vanilla extract

Preheat oven to 350° F. First prepare the crust by combining the graham cracker crumbs, ½ cup sugar, and butter in a medium mixing bowl and mixing with an electric mixer on low speed. Press the cracker mixture into a 9-inch pie pan and bake for 10 minutes. Remove the crust from the oven and set it aside to cool. Reduce the oven temperature to 300° F.

In a medium size bowl combine the sugar, cornstarch, vanilla, and cocoa and, with an electric mixer, mix in the yolks and milk. Pour the mixture into a medium size saucepan and cook over low heat until it thickens, then pour into the baked pie shell.

Make the meringue by beating the egg whites with a whisk until stiff. Fold the salt, ¼ cup of sugar, and vanilla into the stiff egg whites and pour the meringue over pie. Bake for 15 minutes or until light brown. *Serves 8.*

Cherry Cream Cheese Pie

This recipe calls for a package of cream cheese, but reduced fat cream cheese works just as well.

1 ½ cups graham cracker crumbs
½ cup sugar
½ cup (1 stick) unsalted butter, softened
1 (8-ounce) package cream cheese, softened

1 ½ cups sweetened condensed milk
½ cup fresh lemon juice
1 teaspoon vanilla extract
1 20-ounce can cherry filling

Preheat oven to 350° F. First, prepare crust by combining the graham cracker crumbs, sugar, and butter in a medium mixing bowl and mixing with an electric mixer on low speed until combined. Press the cracker mixture into a 9-inch pie pan and bake for 10 minutes. Remove the crust from oven and set it aside to cool.

In a medium mixing bowl beat the cream cheese with an electric mixer on low speed until light and fluffy. Mix in the milk and lemon juice, then add the vanilla. Pour the filling into the pie shell and top it with the cherry filling. Refrigerate for at least 3 hours before serving. *Serves 8.*

Banana Split Pie

This pie can be made up to 3 hours before serving.

1 ½ cups graham cracker crumbs
½ cup sugar
½ cup (1 stick) unsalted butter
4 cups (about 3 to 4 large
   bananas) sliced bananas

½ cup cubed pineapple
2 cups Cool Whip
½ cup pecans, chopped
1 ½ cups fresh cherries, pitted

Preheat oven to 350° F. First, prepare the crust by combining the graham cracker crumbs, sugar, and butter in a medium mixing bowl and mixing with an electric mixer on low speed. Press the cracker mixture into a 9-inch pie pan and bake for 10 minutes. Remove the crust from the oven and set aside to cool. Spread bananas evenly in the bottom of the cooled pie shell, followed by the pineapple. Top with the Cool Whip, pecans, and cherries. Refrigerate until ready to serve. *Serves 8.*

Fresh Rhubarb Pie

Rhubarb is a perennial with long pink to red celery-like stalks and large green leaves. The stalks are extremely tart and are great for baking.

1 ½ cups sugar

¼ cup all-purpose flour

1 teaspoon orange zest

3 cups (about 3 stalks) pink rhubarb, diced into ½-inch pieces

¼ cup (½ stick) unsalted butter, softened

2 unbaked 9-inch pie shells (see recipe on page 65)

Preheat oven to 425° F. In a large mixing bowl, combine the sugar, flour, and orange zest. Add the pink rhubarb and butter and pour the mixture into the pie shell. Cover the pie with the second crust and flute the edges to make a high standing rim. Cut vents on the top and bake for 60 minutes or until the juice from the rhubarb begins to bubble through the vents and the crust turns golden brown. Let cool before serving. *Makes 8 servings.*

Oatmeal Pie

For a spicier flavor, sprinkle the top of this Oatmeal Pie with ground cinnamon and ground cloves before baking.

½ cup (1 stick) unsalted butter
½ cup sugar
½ teaspoon ground cinnamon
¼ teaspoon ground allspice
¼ teaspoon salt
1 cup dark corn syrup

3 large eggs, at room temperature
1 cup quick-cooking rolled oats
1 unbaked 9-inch pie shell (see recipe on page 65)

Preheat oven to 350° F. In a large mixing bowl, cream the butter and sugar with an electric mixer. Add the cinnamon, allspice, and salt. Mix in the corn syrup. Add the eggs one at a time, mixing on low speed after each addition until well blended. Stir in the oats. Pour the filling into pie shell and bake for 60 minutes or until the filling is set. *Makes 8 servings.*

Sweet
Treats

Almost everybody has a sweet tooth and there is nothing better for it than snacking on some homemade caramel candy, pralines, or brown sugar bars. Although sweet treats have been singled out as cavity starters and a cause of weight gain, eating sweet treats in moderation can be a nutritious addition to your diet.

Sweet Spoon Bread

Spoon Bread is a Southern recipe that got its name because it was served with a spoon instead of a fork or a pie cutter. It has the flavor and texture of sweet cornbread.

1 ½ cups cornmeal
1 quart whipping cream
¼ cup (½ stick) salted butter, melted
½ cup sugar

1 teaspoon salt
2 teaspoon baking powder
5 large eggs, well beaten at room temperature
nonstick cooking spray

Preheat oven to 350° F. In a large saucepan, combine the cornmeal and whipping cream and cook over medium heat for 2 minutes, stirring continuously. Remove the cream mixture from the heat and add the butter, sugar, salt, and baking powder. Fold in the eggs. Pour the batter into a 1½-quart baking dish that has been sprayed with nonstick cooking spray. Bake for 60 minutes. *Serves 8.*

Traditional Bread Pudding

A variety of breads can be substituted for the cubed white bread in this recipe, including stale, cubed French bread, cubed wheat bread, or leftover coffee cake (see recipe on page 29).

5 cups stale white bread, cubed
2 ½ cups milk
3 large eggs, well beaten at
   room temperature
¼ cup (½ stick) unsalted butter,
   melted
1 cup sugar

½ teaspoon salt
½ teaspoon ground cinnamon
½ teaspoon ground nutmeg
¼ teaspoon ground allspice
1 cup golden raisins
½ cup pecans, chopped

Preheat oven to 350° F. Soak the bread in the milk in a large bowl for ten minutes. Then add the eggs, butter, sugar, salt, cinnamon, nutmeg, and allspice and mix well with a large wooden spoon. Stir in the raisins and pecans.

Pour the mixture into a 9 × 5 × 2-inch nonstick loaf pan. Place the loaf pan in a 13 × 9-inch baking pan filled with one inch of water and bake for 60 minutes. *Serves 8.*

Fresh Peach Cobbler

◆

This cobbler recipe is very flexible. The peaches can be substituted for apples, oranges, or blackberries.

2 tablespoons cornstarch

1/4 cup light brown sugar

1/2 cup water

4 1/2 cups (about 7 medium peaches) fresh peaches, peeled and sliced

2 tablespoons salted butter, softened

1 tablespoon fresh lemon juice

1/2 cup all-purpose flour, sifted

1/2 cup granulated sugar

1/2 teaspoon baking powder

2 tablespoons unsalted butter, softened

1 large egg, slightly beaten at room temperature

1 tablespoon grandulated sugar (for sprinkling)

1/2 teaspoon ground cinnamon (for sprinkling)

Preheat oven to 400° F. In a large heavy saucepan, combine the cornstarch, brown sugar, and water and mix well. Stir in the peaches and cook over medium heat for about 10 minutes or until the mixture thickens. Remove the peaches from the heat and add the butter and lemon juice. Pour the peach mixture into a nonstick 8-inch round baking dish and set aside.

To make the batter topping, combine the flour, 1/2 cup granulated sugar, baking powder, butter, and egg in a medium mixing bowl and mix with a wire whisk until smooth. Drop the batter by tablespoonfuls over the peach mixture. Sprinkle the batter topping with a mixture of 1 tablespoon granulated sugar and 1/2 teaspoon ground cinnamon and bake for 40 minutes or until the crust turns brown. *Serves 8.*

Fresh Pear Cobbler

Serve this Fresh Pear Cobbler with homemade vanilla ice cream (see page 116).

2 tablespoons cornstarch

¼ cup light brown sugar

½ cup water

4 ½ cups (about 6–7 medium pears) fresh pears, sliced, peeled, and cored

2 ½ tablespoons salted butter, softened

1 tablespoon lemon juice

½ cup all-purpose flour

½ cup granulated sugar

½ teaspoon baking powder

2 tablespoons unsalted butter, softened

1 large egg, slightly beaten at room temperature

1 tablespoon granulated sugar (for sprinkling)

¼ teaspoon ground cloves (for sprinkling)

Preheat oven to 400° F. In a large heavy saucepan, combine the corn starch, brown sugar, and water and mix well. Add the pears and cook over medium heat about 15 minutes or until the mixture thickens. Remove the pears from the heat and add the butter and lemon juice. Pour the pear mixture into an 8-inch nonstick round baking dish.

To make the batter topping, combine the flour, ½ cup granulated sugar, baking powder, butter, and egg in a medium mixing bowl and beat with a spoon until the batter is combined. Drop the batter by tablespoonfuls over the pear mixture, spreading evenly. Sprinkle the top with a mixture of the tablespoon granulated sugar and ground cloves and bake for 50 minutes or until the crust turns brown. *Serves 8.*

Serve this Rice Pudding chilled. Keep refrigerated until ready to serve.

2 cups milk

2 cups cooked white long grain rice

½ cup dark raisins

½ cup sugar

½ teaspoon ground cinnamon

¼ teaspoon ground allspice

1 teaspoon vanilla extract

3 large eggs, well beaten at room temperature

½ teaspoon ground nutmeg

Preheat oven to 350° F. In a medium heavy saucepan, heat the milk until warm but *do not boil*. Remove it from the heat, add the rice, raisins, sugar, cinnamon, allspice, vanilla, and eggs and mix well.

Pour the mixture into a 1½-quart nonstick casserole dish and place the casserole dish in a 13 × 9-inch pan filled with 1 inch of water. Sprinkle the top with nutmeg and bake for 30 minutes. Lightly stir the pudding and bake for an additional 15 minutes or until a knife inserted near the center comes out clean. *Serves 8.*

Banana Nut Pudding

To add a Caribbean flair, use ripe, sliced plantains instead of bananas. However, because plantains are not as sweet as bananas, ⅓ cup of sugar can be added to the recipe.

2 cups milk

1 cup sugar

2 large eggs, well beaten at
    room temperature

3 tablespoons all-purpose flour

1 package instant vanilla
    pudding mix

1 teaspoon vanilla extract

4 cups (about 4 large bananas)
    sliced bananas

3 cups vanilla wafers

¼ cup pecans, chopped

Place the milk in a medium heavy saucepan and bring it to a slow boil over medium heat. Beat in the sugar, eggs, and flour. Add the pudding mix to the milk, stirring continuously until the pudding thickens. Remove the pudding from the heat and add the vanilla.

Layer half of the banana slices in the bottom of a 9-inch round casserole dish. Pour half of the pudding over the bananas. Layer half of the vanilla wafers over the pudding. Add the remainder of the bananas followed by another layer of pudding, then another layer of wafers, and top with the pecans. Refrigerate for at least 2 hours before serving. *Serve 8.*

Strawberry Ice

Instead of Strawberry Ice, watermelon, raspberry or cherry ice can be made, by substituting an equal amount of the desired fruit.

1 ½ pounds ripe strawberries,
 green stems removed
1 cup fresh orange juice

1½ tablespoons powdered gelatin
¼ cup water

Place the strawberries in a food processor and puree. Add the orange juice and set aside for 2 hours to allow the flavor to develop. In a small heavy saucepan, lightly sprinkle the gelatin in the water. Set aside for about 5 minutes or until the gelatin begins to swell and turn soft. Heat the gelatin gently over low heat but *do not boil*, stirring until the gelatin has completely dissolved. Remove it from the heat and let it cool, then add the gelatin to the fruit. Pour the fruit mixture into a medium aluminum bowl, cover it with plastic wrap, and freeze. Every 30 minutes during the first two hours of freezing, stir the mixture vigorously with a wire whisk. *Serves 8.*

Caramel Corn

This Caramel Corn tastes great when it is mixed with an equal amount of regular popcorn.

4 quarts freshly popped corn	*½ cup light corn syrup*
¾ cup (1½ sticks) salted butter	*½ teaspoon salt*
1½ cups light brown sugar, firmly packed	*¼ teaspoon baking soda*

Preheat oven to 250° F. Spread freshly popped corn in a large sheet pan and put it in the oven. In a medium heavy saucepan combine the butter, sugar, syrup, and salt. Place over medium heat, stirring continuously until sugar dissolves. Allow the sugar to boil until it reaches 250° F (about 7 minutes). Remove the sugar from the heat and stir in the baking soda; a syrup will form.

Take the popped corn from the oven and pour the hot caramel mixture over it in a fine stream. Stir the popcorn to coat it with the caramel. Return the popcorn to the oven for about 45 minutes, stirring it every 15 minutes. Cool and serve or store in an airtight container. *Makes about 4 quarts.*

Bourbon Balls

These Bourbon Balls can be prepared and then frozen for up to two months before serving.

2 cups crushed vanilla wafers

1 cup pecans, chopped

2 tablespoons unsweetened cocoa

1 cup granulated sugar

2 tablespoons light corn syrup

½ cup bourbon

¼ cup powdered sugar

(for coating)

Place the crushed vanilla wafers and pecans in a food processor and grind to crumbs. Mix in the cocoa and sugar. Gradually add the corn syrup and bourbon. Mix until it is moist and then shape into small, ½-inch balls. Roll the balls in powdered sugar. Refrigerate for 4 hours before serving. *Makes about 24 small balls.*

Vanilla Fudge

Instead of chopped pecans, chopped hazelnuts or peanuts can be substituted.

4 cups sugar	1 cup pecans, chopped
1 ½ cups evaporated milk	1 cup (2 sticks) salted butter,
2 teaspoons vanilla extract	softened

Combine sugar and milk in a medium heavy saucepan. Cook over medium heat, stirring frequently, until the temperature reaches 236° F., about 10–12 minutes. Remove the mixture from the heat, and add the vanilla, pecans, and butter. Place the saucepan in cold water and stir until the mixture thickens and loses its shiny appearance. Pour the mixture into a buttered 9 × 9-inch buttered pan and cover and refrigerate for 2 hours or until firm. Cut into 2-inch squares when cool. *Makes about 3 pounds.*

Brown Sugar Bars

Keep these brown sugar bars in the refrigerator until ready to serve. They can also be stored frozen for up to two months.

1 cup (2 sticks) salted butter, softened

2 cups dark brown sugar

2 large eggs, well beaten at room temperature

1 ½ teaspoons vanilla extract

2 cups all-purpose flour

½ teaspoon salt

½ teaspoon baking soda

1 (6-ounce) package semi-sweet chocolate chips

Preheat oven to 350° F. In a large mixing bowl, combine the butter, sugar, eggs, vanilla, flour, salt, and baking soda. Using an electric mixer, mix well on medium speed. Spread the mixture in a 10 × 15-inch nonstick baking pan. Sprinkle the chocolate chips on top and bake for 20 minutes. Remove from the oven and let cool for 15 minutes, then chill in the refrigerator for 1 hour before cutting. Cut into 2 × 2-inch bars and serve. *Makes about 35 bars.*

Fruit Cocktail Delight

Fresh seasonal fruits, such as seedless grapes, cherries, cubed pineapple, cubed peaches, and cubed pears can be used instead of canned fruit cocktail.

4 cups crushed vanilla wafers

4 cups canned fruit cocktail, drained

3 cups Cool Whip

½ cup walnuts

Layer the bottom of a 10-inch round dessert plate with crushed vanilla wafers. Layer on ½ of the fruit, then ½ of the Cool Whip. Repeat the process and sprinkle the nuts on top. Refrigerate for one hour before serving. *Serves 8.*

Strawberry-Lemon Whip

If desired, add about 1½ tablespoons of Grand Marnier to the strawberry-lemon mixture before beating it.

2 cups whipping cream
½ cup powdered sugar, sifted
1 cup fresh lemon juice
¼ cup lemon zest

2 tablespoons condensed milk
8 large fresh strawberries
(for garnish)

Combine the cream, sugar, lemon juice, lemon zest, and milk in a large, chilled mixing bowl. Beat the mixture with an electric mixer on medium speed until combined and thick. Divide the mixture among eight 6-ounce dessert glasses and chill until ready to serve. Top each with a strawberry before serving. *Serve 8.*

Fried Apples

These fried apples taste great with Sweet Spoon Bread (see page 93).

½ cup sugar

½ teaspoon ground cinnamon

¼ teaspoon ground nutmeg

½ cup (1 stick) salted butter, softened

5 large apples, peeled, cored, and sliced into ½-inch-thick rings

In a medium mixing bowl, combine the sugar, cinnamon, and nutmeg. Heat the butter in a heavy frying pan over medium heat. Add the apple rings and half of the sugar mixture. Cook for about 4 minutes on one side. Turn the apples over and sprinkle the remainder of the sugar mixture on them. Continue to cook the apples until they become transparent. Serve hot. *Makes about 6–8 servings.*

Sweet Potato Roll

This Sweet Potato Roll can be prepared and stored in the freezer for at least two weeks before serving.

1 cup self-rising flour
1 cup mashed cooked sweet potatoes
1 cup granulated sugar
1 teaspoon vanilla extract
5 eggs, slightly beaten at room temperature

4 ounces cream cheese, softened
4 ounces Cool Whip
¼ cup powdered sugar
¼ teaspoon ground allspice
1 tablespoon vanilla extract
1 cup pecans, chopped

Preheat oven to 325° F. In a medium mixing bowl, combine the flour, sweet potato, sugar, vanilla, and eggs, mix with an electric mixer until well combined. Pour the batter into a 9 × 12-inch non-stick cookie sheet and bake for 20 minutes, *being careful not to burn it*. After removing it from the oven, run a spatula under the cake to make sure it doesn't stick to the pan. Let it cool completely.

In a separate medium mixing bowl, mix the cream cheese, Cool Whip, sugar, allspice, and vanilla with an electric mixer. Spread on top of the cooled cake and sprinkle with pecans. Roll it up beginning on one 12-inch side of the rectangle. Wrap the roll with plastic wrap first then with foil and freeze for at least 4 hours before serving. *Serves 4–6.*

Pineapple Treat

If desired, add about ¼ cup salted, shelled roasted peanuts to the pineapple mixture before baking. This will give the dish a nutty, sweet, and savory taste.

4 ½ cups fresh bread crumbs
3½ cups fresh pineapple cubes
4 large eggs, beaten at room
  temperature

1 ½ cups sugar
½ cup (1 stick) salted butter,
  melted

Preheat oven to 350° F. In a large mixing bowl, toss the bread crumbs and pineapple together. Place the pineapple in a buttered 2-quart baking dish. Using an electric mixer, beat the eggs, sugar, and butter in a small mixing bowl until fluffy and light. Pour over the pineapple. Bake for 30 minutes or until set and the top turns slightly brown. *Serves 8.*

Chocolate Pears

White chocolate can be substituted for the semi-sweet chocolate this recipe calls for.

4 cups water

1 cup sugar

1 tablespoon almond extract

6 whole pears with stems intact, peeled

6 ounces semi-sweet chocolate, melted

Put the water, sugar, and almond extract into a large heavy saucepan and bring to a simmer over medium heat. Cut a thin slice from the base of each pear and stand the pears up in the saucepan. Simmer the pears for 10 minutes or until they are tender. Lift the pears out of the liquid and place them into a shallow bowl. Discard the liquid. While the pears are still hot, pour enough of the melted chocolate over each pear to cover the surface. Set aside to cool for 20 minutes. *Serves 6.*

Sweet Potato Pudding

This sweet potato pudding is fluffy and full of flavor, much like a souffle.

- 5 large eggs, slightly beaten at room temperature
- 1 cup (2 sticks) salted butter, softened
- ½ cup light brown sugar
- 4 cups peeled sweet potatoes, cooked and mashed

- ¼ cup all-purpose flour
- 2 cups milk
- 1 teaspoon ground allspice
- 2 tablespoons salted butter
- 1 tablespoon sugar

Preheat oven to 350° F. Place the eggs, 1 cup butter, sugar, sweet potatoes, flour, milk, and allspice in a food processor and mix until the texture is light and fluffy. Rub a 3-quart casserole baking dish with 2 tablespoons of butter and sprinkle the sides with sugar. Pour the sweet potato mixture into the buttered baking casserole. Bake for 60 minutes or until set. *Serves 8.*

Turtle Candy

This delicious candy will keep in the freezer for up to 2 months.

4 ½ cups sugar
1 ½ cups evaporated milk
½ cup (1 stick) salted butter
4 cups pecan halves

1 12-ounce bag semi-sweet
  chocolate chips
2 cups marshmallow cream

Combine sugar, milk, and butter in a large heavy saucepan and cook on medium heat until it comes to a full boil, stirring continuously. Remove the mixture from the heat and add the pecans and chocolate chips. Stir until the chips melt. Add the marshmallow cream and continue to stir until well mixed. Drop by tablespoonfuls, spaced about 1 inch apart, onto a cookie sheet lined with wax paper. Refrigerate for 2 hours before serving. *Makes about 4 pounds.*

Pralines

Pralines were local favorites in New Orleans that eventually became popular across the country. Nearly every African-American household has its own version of a praline recipe. This one is from my family.

½ cup sugar

1 cup evaporated milk

1 ½ cups sugar

2 cups pecans, chopped

1 tablespoon salted butter

1 ½ teaspoons vanilla extract

Place ½ cup sugar in a medium heavy saucepan. Carmelize the sugar over medium heat, stirring continuously. Add the milk and let the mixture boil for 3 minutes. Stir in 1½ cups sugar and the pecans. Remove the mixture from the heat and let it cool for 10 minutes. Add the butter and vanilla and beat well. Drop by table-spoonfuls, spaced ½ inch apart, onto a cookie sheet lined with wax paper. Let the pralines set for about 1 hour before serving. *Makes about 2 pounds.*

Chocolate Fudge

To create a marbled look, use 6 ounces of semi-sweet chocolate chips and 6 ounces of white chocolate chips instead of the 12 ounces of semi-sweet chocolate chips called for.

3 cups sugar

¼ cup (½ stick) salted butter

1 cup evaporated milk

1 12-ounce bag semi-sweet
  chocolate chips

½ cup marshmallow cream

1 ½ cups walnuts, chopped

1 teaspoon vanilla extract

Combine the sugar, butter, and milk in a large heavy saucepan. Over high heat, bring to a rolling boil, stirring continuosly, and continue to boil the mixture for 5 minutes. Remove the mixture from the heat and add the chocolate chips, stirring until melted. Add marshmallow cream, walnuts, and vanilla. Mix until well blended. Pour into a buttered, greased 13 × 9-inch baking pan. Let it cool for 15 minutes, then refrigerate for 2 hours or until firm. Cut it into 2 × 3-inch squares. *Makes about 2½ pounds.*

Caramel Candy

For a nuttier flavor, toast the pecans in a 325° F. oven for 5 minutes, shaking them constantly, before adding them to the saucepan.

2 ½ cups sugar

1 cup evaporated milk

2 tablespoons vanilla extract

1 cup pecans, chopped

Mix the sugar and milk in a large heavy saucepan. Over high heat, bring to a boil, stirring continuously. Remove the mixture from the heat and add the vanilla and pecans. Beat well and pour into a buttered, greased 8 × 9-inch baking dish. Let the candy cool and cut into small pieces and wrap in plastic wrap. *Makes about 2 pounds.*

Peach Mousse

Instead of peaches, an equal amount of mangos can be substituted.

3 ½ cups fresh peaches, peeled
   and sliced
1 cup sugar

1 tablespoon fresh lemon juice
2 teaspoons vanilla extract
1 ½ cups heavy cream, whipped

Place the peaches, sugar, lemon juice, and vanilla into a food processor and blend on medium speed until texture is smooth. Fold in the whipped cream and pour into a large bowl. Cover the mousse tightly with plastic wrap and freeze for about 3 hours. Serve in sherbet or parfait glasses. *Makes about 2 quarts.*

Homemade Vanilla Ice Cream

If desired, about 2 cups of fresh fruit, such as sliced strawberries, can be added.

1 quart milk	8 egg yolks, at room temperature
1 pint whipping cream	1 tablespoon vanilla extract
2 cups sugar	½ teaspoon nutmeg

Place the milk and cream in a large heavy saucepan and bring to a boil over medium heat. In a large aluminum bowl beat the sugar and yolks together until light and fluffy. Pour the heated milk into the yolk mixture. Fold in the vanilla and nutmeg and set aside to cool. Seal tightly with plastic wrap and freeze for at least 4 hours. *Makes about 2 quarts.*

Peanut Brittle

This Peanut Brittle makes a great present and, if stored in a cool place or in the freezer, it can last for up to one month.

1 ½ cups sugar
½ cup light corn syrup
¼ cup water

½ teaspoon salt
2 cups raw peanuts
1 teaspoon baking soda

Place all the ingredients, except the baking soda, into a large heavy skillet. Simmer over medium heat, stirring continuously with a wooden spoon, until it smells scorched (about 10 minutes). Take the mixture off the heat and add the baking soda, continuing to stir. Spread the mixture on a buttered cookie sheet and let it cool. Once cooled, break up and serve or store. *Makes about 2 pounds.*

Brownies

You can substitute an equal amount of dark or golden raisins for the walnuts.

1 ½ cups (3 sticks) unsalted
    butter, softened
1 cup sugar
2 teaspoons vanilla extract
2 cups all-purpose flour
1 ½ teaspoons baking powder

½ teaspoon salt
¾ cup unsweetened cocoa powder
2 large eggs, at room
    temperature
½ cup walnuts, chopped
½ cup semi-sweet chocolate chips

Preheat oven to 350° F. Place the butter and sugar in a medium mixing bowl and mix on low speed with an electric mixer until fluffy. Gradually add the vanilla, flour, baking powder, salt, and cocoa. Mix with an electric mixer until the texture becomes pasty. Add the eggs one at a time. Fold in the walnuts. Spread the mixture in a 9 × 9 × 2-inch nonstick pan. Sprinkle the chocolate chips on top and bake for 20 minutes. Remove the brownies from the oven and let them cool. Cut into 2-inch squares. *Makes about 2 dozen.*

Index

About the Author

Wilbert Jones, the author of the nationally acclaimed *Healthy Soul Food Cookbook*, attended the Ecole de Gastronomique Française Ritz-Escoffier in Paris and was a food scientist at Kraft General Foods. He is the president of Healthy Concepts, Inc., a food consulting company, and teaches seminars and workshops on healthier cooking. *The Healthy Soul Food Cookbook* won the Purple Reflection award from the National Council of Negro Women, one of the oldest women's organizations in America. He lives in Chicago.